THE

KENNEDY LIBRARY

by WILLIAM DAVIS and CHRISTINA TREE

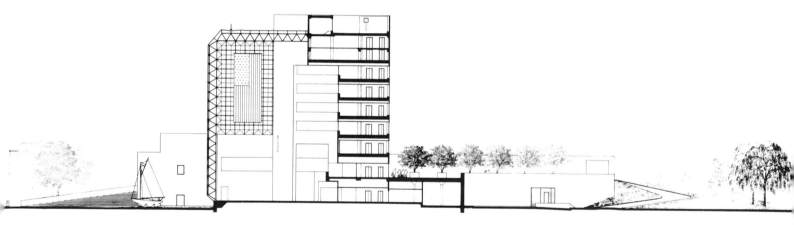

Schiffer Publishing Ltd

Box E, Exton, Pennsylvania 19341

Cover Photograph and Book Design by Steven Carothers.

Copyright © 1980 Schiffer Publishing Limited, Box E, Exton, Pennsylvania 19341. All rights reserved. No part of this book may be reproduced in any form, including photocopy, without written permission from the publisher.

Library of Congress catalog card number: 80-53154

Hard Cover ISBN 0-916838-29-3
Soft Cover ISBN 0-916838-36-6

Printed in the United States of America

For Liam, Timothy and Christopher

Introduction

John F. Kennedy's assassination on November 22, 1963 was one of the most unifying events in modern history. Over the ensuing decade millions of people from throughout the world contributed eighteen million dollars to build his library. Many times that number would be saddened were it any less of a memorial to this particular, widely loved and respected leader.

On the other hand, a presidential library must be more than a memorial. This one is dedicated "to all those who through the art of politics seek a new and better world."

"We are rooted but not anchored in the past," insists Dan Fenn, the Library's director. Fenn sees the captivating presence of John Kennedy as a means of involving visitors in the meaning of the presidency.

The building itself reflects this dual purpose. Architect I. M. Pei feels strongly about John Kennedy. He deliberately submerges you for an hour in the sights and sounds of the early sixties, then permits you to surface into the airy emptiness of the one hundred and ten foot high glass pavilion, a space which invites you to fill it with your own thoughts.

For Pei, this combination of action (the lively exhibit area) and reflection (the pavilion) suggests the character of John Kennedy.

It was because Kennedy himself was a sailor, one who called Americans to set sail with him, that Pei has also designed a building suggestive of both a stark light house and a thrusting boat. Its literal center is occupied, however, not by a bust of John F. Kennedy but by a replica of the desk at which his presidential decisions were made.

Should we put a man on the moon? How does one most effectively go about integrating public housing? How can one human being deal with the responsibility for hundreds of lives lost in the Bay of Pigs disaster, let alone with the burden of fending off nuclear war?

In 1961 the polls revealed that eighty-three percent of Americans thought their president was doing a good job, a level of confidence unequaled since. The very opposition encountered in getting this building built reflects, to a degree, the declining respect in recent decades for the office of president.

Kennedy was the first president to request that his library be linked to a university in order that he might use it—after retiring from eight years in office, aged fifty-one—partly as a podium from which to convey a better appreciation of the presidency and of the political process both to students and the public in general.

As envisioned back in 1964 the Kennedy Library was to be adjacent to Harvard University and to incorporate an Institute of Politics, a place in which active statesmen could teach, occasionally lecturing the public as well. Today this institute does exist but as an integral part of Harvard University's graduate school of government, itself renamed to honor Kennedy and occupying a part of the Cambridge site which—for ten years—was slated for the entire library.

The long, complicated story about how the Kennedy Library itself got from Cambridge to Dorchester is detailed in this book. The point is that by the mid-seventies, when local opposition forced the Kennedy Library Corporation to search out another site, the institute was already a part of Harvard. It was actually touch and go for a while whether the archives too might remain in Cambridge while the museum was floated off to some less trafficked place.

The decision to keep the archives and museum together and adjacent to a university was itself a commitment to animating the museum through ongoing research and to using the total Library—the archives, the exhibits, the building itself and the staff—as one powerful resource in teaching American politics, government and recent history.

It should be remembered that when this magnificent building was finally dedicated in October, 1979, that the Library's archival staff had already been at work for more than a decade, processing millions of pages of documents, some one hundred and fifteen thousand photos and more than six million feet of film, a collection which includes papers of many outstanding men of Kennedy's day. (Ernest Hemingway's papers, for instance, are here.) There are also eleven hundred oral histories, interviews with Kennedy associates ranging from Boston pols to heads of state.

Of the six other presidential libraries this is at once the best sited for students (it is accessible by public transit from forty-six colleges and universities) and general visitors (it is the only one to be found in a major metropolitan area). In its first six months, the Kennedy Library recorded more than three hundred thousand visitors, establishing it as one of New England's leading sites to see as well as the most visited of the six other presidential libraries.

Another of the Kennedy Library's unique distinctions is that it is the only presidential library in which the man it is dedicated to neither had a post-White House office nor was buried there. The building, in other words, never knew John Kennedy's physical presence.

That void has had to be filled by the archives which document his administration, the museum which illustrates the highpoints of his personal and presidential life, and the involvement of those who knew John Kennedy well and continue to be concerned about the needs and problems of America that concerned him. The Kennedy Library Corporation, composed of members of the Kennedy family and many former associates of JFK, no longer owns the library building and is not responsible for its operation, but continues to be keenly interested in it and its projects.

In its efforts to reach out to the public and to make all of its resources available for those who want to learn more about American government, the Kennedy Library is doing exactly what it was meant to do.

"Not just a library, but an active institution," is the way Robert Kennedy described the memorial he wanted built to his brother.

"It should be a place," he said, "not just for scholars and sightseers, but one where all sorts of people could learn about the art of government John Kennedy exemplified."

He would be pleased, we think.

C.M.T. / W.A.D.

Table of Contents

JFK at White House press conference.

(Photo: John Fitzgerald Kennedy Library)

A Man, His Brother, and Their Times

"This library is dedicated to the memory of John Fitzgerald Kennedy, thirty-fifth president of the United States of America, and to all those who through the art of politics seek a new and better world."

That inscription on the wall of its entrance lobby both sets the tone and implies the purpose of the Kennedy Library—both unlike those of other presidential libraries. More than just a memorial to JFK, the monumental building named for him is more importantly a place where anyone from school boy to scholar can come to study the American political process, particularly as illustrated by the life and career of President Kennedy.

The museum area, occupying the lower level of a building largely given over to records and research, presents JFK's life in a series of exhibits that treat him not only as a great president and an historical figure, but as a case history of American politics—a unique individual, but very much a man of his times and nation.

Designed by Chermayeff & Geismar Associates, a New York graphics firm which designed the American Bicentennial symbol and has produced many industrial exhibitions, museum displays are carefully designed and crafted to give the visitor a series of physical, emotional, and intellectual experiences through advanced multi-media techniques that appeal to the senses as well as the mind.

A visit to the library begins with a thirty minute film on the life of President Kennedy, shown in one of two two-hundred-and-fifty seat eliptically shaped theaters.

Produced and directed by Charles Guggenheim, a distinguished documentary film maker who has won two Motion Picture Academy "Oscars," it is entitled simply "John F. Kennedy, 1917–1963." Making the film was anything but simple, however, since nearly three years of research were involved and eight hundred thousand feet of motion picture film were screened, thousands of still photographs studied and the best—much of it never released before—distilled into a half hour documentary that movingly covers the highlights of President Kennedy's life.

A longer film could easily have been made, of course, and the first draft of the JFK film was around nine hours long. What remains after artful compression and editing is a memorable portrait in black and white—color film was not widely used for news coverage in Kennedy's time—covering the highlights of his life from childhood in suburban Boston through his days in the White House.

The last, and most dramatic, part of the film deals with JFK's fiercely fought campaign for the presidency and some of the highlights and crises of his presidential years. Few presidents have been as open to the media as Kennedy—he was the first to allow filming in the oval office of the White House—and the filming has some remarkably intimate footage.

Intended as an orientation film, one that would inform the young while rekindling the memories of Kennedy contemporaries, the film is quite even handed in its treatment. The Bay of Pigs incident, for instance, is referred to by narrator David Wayne as "His first and worst mistake."

When the lights come on and the audience exits into the lower level of the building, it is safe to say that virtually all of them are carrying the memory of John Fitzgerald Kennedy with them. They are psychologically prepared, in other words, to tour the museum.

The museum, or exhibit area, covers eighteen thousand square feet and displays three hundred-and-fifteen objects, six hundred documents, seven hundred-and-fifty

The different faces of John Kennedy greet visitors when they enter the lobby of the Kennedy Library. Above the photo murals is written: "This library is dedicated to the memory of John Fitzgerald Kennedy, 35th president of the United States of America, and to all those who through the art of politics seek a new and better world."

JFK library visitors wait to see the orientation film, work of prizewinning film maker Charles Guggenheim, entitled simply: "John F. Kennedy, 1917–1963." The film, which begins with Kennedy's funeral, traces his life from childhood through the White House years, and represents a distillation of eight hundred thousand feet of motion picture film and thousands of still photographs.

10

Ask not what your country can do for you—
ask what you can do for your country.
Inaugural Address, 1961

We can help make the world safe for diversity.
For, in the final analysis, our most basic
common link is that we all inhabit this small planet.
We all breathe the same air.
We all cherish our children's future.
And we all are mortal.
Commencement Address at American University, 1963

Control of arms is a mission that we undertake
particularly for our children and our grandchildren...
they have no lobby in Washington.
Statement on securing world peace, 1963

Our deep spiritual confidence that this nation
will survive the perils of today...compels us
to invest in our nation's future, to consider
and meet our obligations to our children
and the numberless generations that will follow.
Special Message to the Congress on Conservation, 1962

Our goal is not the victory of might
but the vindication of right—
not peace at the expense of freedom,
but both peace *and* freedom,
here in this hemisphere,
and, we hope, around the world,
God willing, that goal will be achieved.
Report on the Soviet Arms Build-up in Cuba, 1962

We love our country, not for what it was,
though it has always been great—
not for what it is, though of this we are
deeply proud—but for what it someday can,
and, through the efforts of us all, someday will be.
Address to the National Industrial Conference Board, 1961

When I ran for the Presidency of the United States,
I knew that this country faced serious challenges,
but I could not realize—nor could any man realize
who does not bear the burdens of this office—
how heavy and constant would be those burdens.
Radio and TV Report on the Berlin Crisis, 1961

*Panels bearing some of JFK's most
famous quotations decorate the walls of
the museum. Inspiring JFK quotes are an
integral part of the library exhibition area.
This group of Kennedy quotations contains
the oft quoted line from his inaugural address:
"Ask not what your country can do for
you—ask what you can do for your country."*

The stories of past courage...can teach,
they can offer hope, they can provide inspiration.
But they cannot supply courage itself.
For this each man must look into his own soul.
Profiles in Courage, 1956

When at some future date the high court
of history sits in judgment on each of us...
our success or failure...will be measured
by the answers to four questions:
First, were we truly men of courage...?
Secondly, were we truly men of judgment...?
Third, were we truly men of integrity...?
Finally, were we truly men of dedication?
Address to the Massachusetts State Legislature, 1961

Let us never negotiate out of fear.
But let us never fear to negotiate.
Inaugural Address, 1961

My fellow Americans, let us take that first step.
Let us...step back from the shadows of war
and seek out the way of peace.
And if that journey is a thousand miles,
or even more, let history record that we,
in this land, at this time, took the first step.
Radio and TV Address on Nuclear Test Ban Treaty, 1963

photographs (many shown publicly for the first time) and uses twenty-two mural size back-lit transparencies. As they walk into the exhibit area, most visitors are brought up short by one of these transparencies—a striking photograph of Joseph P. and Rose Kennedy with all nine of their children, taken in 1938 when he was U. S. Ambassador to Great Britain.

These transparency murals are typical of the contemporary exhibition techniques used in the museum, including a variety of multimedia techniques such as audio and video tracks, rear projection slide programs, telespot message boards, and the like.

Visitors circulate clockwise, through chronological theme areas that revolve around a central area containing a replica of President Kennedy's White House desk first used by Rutherford B. Hayes—who was presented it by Queen Victoria—and perimeter windows displaying documents relating to twelve presidential functions.

But, it is the theme areas that are the core of the exhibit. Running above the exhibit cases is a "Time Line," a list of national and international events that provides a frame of reference for occurences in the lives of members of the Kennedy Family. For instance, in 1917—the year John F. Kennedy was born—the time line notes that Puerto Ricans also were granted U.S. citizenship, a revolution broke out in Russia, and America entered World War I.

The time line also helps make the point that the museum is trying to put John and Robert Kennedy in political as well as historical perspective. It begins in 1840—nine years before Patrick Kennedy, JFK's great-grandfather, left Ireland for America—with the election of William Henry Harrison. The use of advertising and electioneering techniques,

An ambassador's family. This famous photo, showing the entire Kennedy family, was taken in London just before the outbreak of World War II when Joseph P. Kennedy, Sr. was United States ambassador to the Court of St. James. From left: Eunice, John, Rosemary, Jean, Ambassador Kennedy, Edward, Mrs. Rose Kennedy, Joseph, Jr., Patricia, Robert, and Kathleen. (Credit: Dorothy Wilding)

such as the famous slogan "Tippecanoe and Tyler, too!" made this the first "modern" presidential campaign. The theme areas begin, however, with the arrival in Boston of the Irish—and the Kennedys.

FORMATIVE YEARS

"John F. Kennedy's great-grandparents emigrated from Ireland to the United States, moving with thousands of their fellow countrymen away from poverty and hunger toward the new world of hope," a caption notes at the start of an exhibit that includes photos of wretched looking Irish peasants before a thatched hut, and—representing the prejudice that greeted them in the New World—anti-Irish cartoons and a "Positively No Irish Need Apply" sign.

Highlights of the Kennedy-Nixon debates are shown on a TV monitor in the museum area. JFK's cool, controlled performance during the debates was a major factor in his victory in 1960 over then Vice President Nixon.

A "time line" running above the exhibits, helps put JFK and RFK's lives and careers in historic perspective.

John F. Kennedy's battered old Underwood typewriter.

A ship model of a French frigate of the 18th Century, part of JFK's collection.

The camera used by Jacqueline Bouvier when she was an inquiring photographer for the Washington Times Herald is one of the exhibits in the section on JFK's early political career. She was working as a photographer when she met Kennedy, then a congressman, in 1951. They were married two years later.

This was the kind of silver service used at the "Kennedy Teas" presided over by Mrs. Rose Kennedy and JFK's sisters in the 1952 campaign against incumbent United States Senator Henry Cabot Lodge. Some seventy-five thousand women attended the teas and JFK won the election over the favored Lodge by seventy thousand, seven hundred and thirty-seven votes.

(Photo: S. Carothers)

This tattered flag, which once flew over it, is all that remains of JFK's World War II boat, PT-109. A member of the crew mailed it home to his mother just before the engagement in which the ship was sunk by the Japanese. JFK's courage won him a medal but he also suffered injuries that were to plague him for the rest of his life.

Gifts that JFK received during his term of office and some of the elaborate gowns worn at White House functions are among the most carefully studied exhibits.

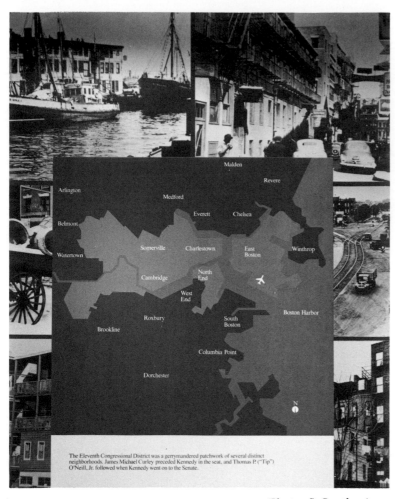

The Eleventh Congressional District was a gerrymandered patchwork of several distinct neighborhoods. James Michael Curley preceded Kennedy in the seat, and Thomas P. ("Tip") O'Neill, Jr. followed when Kennedy went on to the Senate.

(Photo: S. Carothers)

Photographs and a map show the gerry-mandered, ethnically diverse 11th Massachusetts Congressional District where John Kennedy launched his political career in 1946. Despite charges that he was "a carpetbagger," JFK bested a large field to win the seat in the United States House of Representatives previously held by the colorful James Michael Curley.

This quotation from his inaugural address is on the wall of the pavilion, a dramatic room designed by architect I. M. Pei to contrast with the dimly lit museum area—and to allow thoughts to soar.

All this will not be finished
in the first one hundred days.
Nor will it be finished
in the first one thousand days,
nor in the life
of this Administration,
nor even perhaps
in our lifetime on this planet
But let us begin.

Inaugural Address

Photographs of the rolling green landscape of rural Ireland and the humble holding in the hamlet of Dunganstown, just outside New Ross in County Wexford, illustrate what Patrick Kennedy left behind. A cooper's tool shows the trade he practiced in East Boston.

"When my great-grandfather left here to become a cooper in East Boston, he carried nothing with him except two things: a strong religious faith and a strong desire for liberty," President Kennedy said when he visited New Ross in 1963.

Both the Kennedys and the Fitzgeralds, the president's mother's family—who also hailed from Wexford—had to work hard to maintain large families but eventually prospered.

Photographs, documents and memorabilia—such as the Fitzgerald family Bible on which JFK took his inaugural oath—tell the story of their rise from poverty to relative affluence in a generation.

Both of JFK's grandparents—John F. "Honey Fitz" Fitzgerald and Patrick J. Kennedy—were handsome youths, judging by their photographs, and turned into energetic, self-made men who yanked themselves up by hard work and the sturdy bootstrap of Boston politics.

Thomas Fitzgerald, a grocer in Boston's North End, died in 1885, leaving nine motherless children. The third son, John Francis Fitzgerald—the grandfather for whom JFK was named—left Harvard Medical School and went to work to hold the family together. He worked as a customs clerk and in the insurance business but his outgoing nature and quick tongue made a political career almost inevitable. "Honey Fitz," so called because of his silver tongued—and honey mouthed—orations became a state senator, U. S. representative, and one of Boston's most memorable mayors.

"Honey Fitz' " theme song was "Sweet Adeline," a ditty he sang in public thousands of times. Sheet music for the song is displayed with other "Honey Fitz" campaign memorabilia.

(Photo: John Fitzgerald Kennedy Library)

John F. Fitzgerald, the maternal grandfather for whom President Kennedy was named. Forced to leave Harvard Medical School when his father died, he worked briefly as a customs clerk and insurance agent but his gregarious nature and the oratorial gifts that won him the nickname "Honey Fitz" naturally propelled him into politics. He served in the Massachusetts State Senate, the United States House of Representatives, and was a longtime and colorful mayor of Boston best remembered for singing "Sweet Adeline," his theme song, on every possible occasion.

18

(Photo: John Fitzgerald Kennedy Library)

President Kennedy's maternal grandfather, John F. "Honey Fitz" Fitzgerald, was a natural subject for Boston political cartoonists. Short in stature but large in enthusiasm, he was known as "the little general" and often depicted as Napoleon. Despite occasional retirement announcements, he was a perennial candidate for public office and even in 1937, when he was seventy-four years old, was leading a drive for a "Bigger, Better, Busier" Boston and New England.

These cartoons by "Norman" are from the old Boston Post, which was usually sympathetic to "Honey Fitz" and other Irish-American politicians.

(Photo: John Fitzgerald Kennedy Library)

Patrick J. Kennedy, JFK's paternal grandfather, in his prime. Known simply but respectfully in Boston political circles as "P.J." he started life humbly as a longshoreman in East Boston. Turning to bar keeping, he eventually owned several saloons, a prosperous wholesale liquor business, and founded a bank. He also served six terms in the Massachusetts legislature and was considered one of the "kingmakers" of the Democratic Party.

At the age of twenty-five, Joseph Kennedy was running the Columbia Trust Company of Boston and was considered the youngest bank president in the country.

A twenty year old Jack Kennedy practices the art of street juggling on a Belgian pavement during a European trip in 1937.

Joseph P. Kennedy, Sr. was only an average student at Boston Latin School but was president of his class and as shown here in the uniform of captain of the school cadet regiment, led Latin to victory in the annual citywide drill competition.

The comfortable, rambling Fitz-
gerald home in West Concord, Mass.
The Fitzgeralds later moved back to
Boston.

(Photo: John Fitzgerald Kennedy Library)

The handsome, shingled house in Winthrop, Massachusetts, just outside Boston,
which Patrick J. Kennedy purchased after the family left East Boston.

(Photo: John Fitzgerald Kennedy Library)

John Fitzgerald Kennedy, 35th President of the United States, was born in this house at 83 Beals Street, in the Boston suburb of Brookline. In this house John F. Kennedy learned the basic skills each man must learn: to walk, to talk and laugh and pray. In 1921, when he was four years old, the family moved. The house was repurchased by the Kennedy family in 1966 and has been restored to its appearance in 1917. NPS Photo by Richard Frear.

JFK's paternal grandfather, Patrick J. Kennedy, also dropped out of school (high school, not Harvard) to work as a stevedore on the Boston docks. Later, he owned a tavern—a saloon keeper was an influential person in those days—and started a bank in East Boston. He also served seven terms in the Massachusetts legislature and was known as a political kingmaker.

A good businessman, he promoted his wholesale liquor company by, among other things, distributing corkscrews branded "P. J. Kennedy," one of which is displayed. (In Boston politics, he was referred to simply, but respectfully, as "P. J."). A photograph of the substantial, turreted Victorian home of the Kennedys in suburban Winthrop, Massachusetts, gives a good idea of how far, and also how fast the family had come in just one generation from a mud-walled cabin in Wexford.

For many visitors to the Kennedy library, particularly those of the older generation—JFK's contemporaries—these family mementoes are fascinating and absorbing, something like being allowed to roam through the Kennedy Family's collective attic.

And that is where many of the items exhibited actually came from. Curator Dave Powers, an aide and associate of President Kennedy from his first congressional campaign in 1946, solicited photos, documents, and artifacts from Kennedy family members— and searched some out himself. "I spent so much time in the President's mother's attic that she must have thought that I was winterizing the place," he said.

Among the family treasures shown to visitors are the Kennedy christening dress—a gift from grandmother Mary Hickey Kennedy in which JFK and his brothers and sisters were all christened—diaries, scrapbooks, sailing trophies and personal letters. Among these is one entitled "A Plea for A Raise" which twelve year old Jack Kennedy "dedicated" to his father.

The young JFK noted that his allowance was forty cents and "this I used for aeroplanes and other playthings of childhood."

The young Jack Kennedy made a rather winsome cop on the beat. This photo was taken outside of his birthplace in Brookline, Massachusetts.

24

But, he went on: "...now I am a scout and I put away my childish things. Before, I would spend twenty of my forty cents and in five minutes would have empty pockets and nothing to gain and twenty cents to lose. When I am a scout I have to buy canteens, haversacks, blankets, searchlights, poncho, things that will last for years and I can always use it while I can't use a chocolate marshmallow sundae with vanilla ice cream and so I put in my plea for a raise of thirty cents for me to pay my own way more around."

He concluded with a "finis" and signed it "John Fitzgerald Francis Kennedy," apparently hoping that his recently acquired confirmation name would add weight to his appeal. It worked anyway, Joseph P. Kennedy granted the raise—and saved the letter.

The elder Kennedy was himself precocious in financial matters. When he took over the Columbia Trust Company of Boston at the age of twenty-five he became the youngest bank president in the nation and, as photographs show, certainly one of the handsomest and most self-assured of any age.

He had attended the Boston Latin School, a public high school founded in 1635 and known for high academic standards, as well as an unofficial but long-standing relationship with Harvard College. According to Boston tradition, Harvard was created to give Latin graduates someplace to go to. For many an immigrant's son or grandson, a Latin School diploma was the passport to success. ("Honey Fitz" went there, too.)

In full football regalia, JFK—front row, second from right—poses with classmates at the Dexter School. He also played football at his preparatory school, Choate, and while playing football as a freshman at Harvard ruptured a disk in his back, an injury that almost kept him out of the service when World War II broke out.

Joseph Kennedy was only an average student at Latin, but demonstrated leadership as president of his class, commander of the school cadet regiment, and captain of the baseball team. He batted .580 in 1907, and posed proudly with fellow players for the team photo.

Rose Fitzgerald was a devout but vivacious girl who graduated from Dorchester High School—not far from the site of the Kennedy Library—receiving her diploma from the mayor: her father. In 1908, she spent the summer in Europe with her parents, staying behind with her sister Agnes for a year to attend a convent school in Holland.

She was considered the belle of Boston's Irish Catholic society—a glance at her photographs makes it understandable why—and at her debut in 1911, some four hundred and fifty guests (including the entire city council) crowded into the Fitzgerald home. In 1914, she became engaged to Kennedy whom she had met at an outing at Old Orchard Beach, Maine.

Their wedding took place in the private chapel of William Cardinal O'Connell, archbishop of Boston. One of her admirers was Sir Thomas Lipton, famous America's Cup yachtsman and tea merchant, who sent a congratulatory letter and a set of china decorated with the emblem of his yacht "Erin," both of which are displayed.

After honeymooning in West Virginia (a state that would play a crucial part in the life of their second son), the couple settled into a spacious middle class home at 83 Beals Street, in Brookline, a Boston suburb. The house is now a national historic site administered by the National Park Service.

Here, on May 29, 1917, John Fitzgerald Kennedy was born—the first American president born in the 20th Century. Life in the steadily growing Kennedy family was lively and busy, filled with sports, study, and family outings. The exhibits—scrapbooks, diaries, and photographs—reflect this extraordinary "vigor."

Joseph Kennedy was appointed ambassador to the Court of St. James by Franklin Roosevelt. The Kennedy family made an enormous impression on the British. The fact that Mrs. Kennedy kept a card file on her children seemed the epitome of American efficiency in England.

"When Joe became ambassador... the English press treated my card file as a phenomenon of the magnitude of Henry Ford's assembly line. My dutifully kept box of file cards thus became a symbol of American efficiency," Rose Kennedy recalled in 1974, "Actually, it had just been a matter of Kennedy desperation."

But, most visitors to the Kennedy Library who look at Mrs. Kennedy's battered and well-stuffed file card box sense the crammed life it reflects, and are as impressed as the British journalists of the 1930's.

John Kennedy briefly attended Canterbury School in Connecticut (the only Catholic school he ever went to) and then in 1931 transferred to Choate. A much used Choate desk serves to display a JFK school essay on the theme of "justice" showing the birth of a passionate concern for social justice. Some of his favorite books are exhibited including "King Arthur and His Knights," demonstrating an early interest in the "Camelot" legend.

His father's position as U. S. ambassador to Britain at the outbreak of World War II gave JFK a unique vantage point from which to study international affairs—and he made good use of it.

He traveled extensively around Europe, and his notes and albums from these trips are displayed. After the war broke out, his father sent him to Scotland to interview American survivors of the British ship "Athenia," for an embassy report. He drew on some of these personal experiences, as well as advice from his father, for his Harvard honors thesis "Appeasement at Munich," later published —and well recieved—as "Why England Slept."

The war also had tragic consequences for the Kennedy family. The eldest son, Joseph P. Kennedy, Jr., volunteered for a perilous mission: to fly a remote controlled plane to a German rocket base in France. But, before

The growing Kennedy family. Taken at the Kennedy compound in Hyannisport in 1928. Edward was not yet born, making Jean the baby.

they could bail out the plane blew up, killing the crewmen. (As a seventeen year old seaman, Robert Kennedy served on the newly-commissioned destroyer "Joseph P. Kennedy, Jr.")

Kathleen Kennedy worked with the Red Cross in England and was married to a young English aristocrat, Lord Hartington, who was killed with the Coldstream Guards in Belgium—just a month after the death of Joe Jr. (Kathleen survived the war but was killed in a plane crash in 1948.)

The lost Prince. This photograph of Joseph P. Kennedy, Jr. was taken in 1941 at the Squantum Naval Air Training Base in Quincy, Massachusetts, just across the bay from the Kennedy Library site. He volunteered for a perilous mission and was killed when the plane he was flying, to attack a German rocket base in France, accidentally exploded.

(Photo: John Fitzgerald Kennedy Library)

Kathleen "Kick" Kennedy, posing with an obliging rooster at a benefit in England in 1944 while serving as a Red Cross volunteer. Her husband, the Marquis of Hartington was killed in France that year while serving with the Coldstream Guards. Her brother, Joseph, Jr., died a month earlier. She was killed in a plane crash in 1948.

This formal family portrait was released to the press in 1938 when Joseph P. Kennedy was named United States ambassador to Great Britain. To the left of the fireplace, from the left: Joseph, Sr., Patricia, John, Jean, and Eunice. To the right, from the left: Robert, Kathleen, Edward, Rosemary, Joseph, Jr., and Mrs. Rose Kennedy. (Credit: Fabian Bachrach.)

JFK joined the Navy—the obvious choice for someone who loved boats as much as he did—and ended up commanding the legendary PT-109 in the Solomon Islands. In a now famous action, PT-109 sank while engaging the Japanese but Kennedy displayed great coolness and courage and got his crew onto an island where he was able to send a message by native canoe to an Australian coastwatcher who summoned help. (The coconut shell on which he carved his S. O. S. message was one of JFK's prized possessions, and sat on his desk in the oval office of the White House.)

He was awarded the Navy and Marine Corps medal and the Purple Heart, but was modest about his honors. Asked: "How did you become a war hero?" He answered: "It was involuntary. They sank my boat."

Many visitors expect a JFK museum to have the PT-109 on display, and ask where it is. The answer: "It sank to the bottom of the Pacific." There is a scale model of the PT boat which was presented to President Kennedy and the very flag which it was flying the day he took command on April 29, 1943.

JFK had some initial difficulty meeting Navy requirements for enlistment and his wartime experiences severly damaged his health. He injured his back when PT-109 sank, an injury that would plague him for the rest of his life, and a bout of malaria left him emaciated.

"He had scarlet fever when he was very young, and serious back trouble when he was older." Robert Kennedy recalled, "In between he had almost every other conceivable ailment... we use to laugh about the great risk a mosquito took in biting Jack Kennedy—with some of his blood the mosquito was almost sure to die."

But, despite his physical problems, when Jack Kennedy was discharged from the Navy he chose for his career field the rough and tumble one of politics.

This photo, taken in the Solomons in 1943, shows Kennedy at the wheel of PT-109. His explanation of how he became a hero was: "It was involuntary. They sank my boat."

(Photo: *John Fitzgerald Kennedy Library*)

"We don't want the exhibits just to say what we have, we want them to tell what we have to say," said Kennedy Library director Dan Fenn. "We want the library used as a teaching museum—the exhibit on Kennedy's '46 campaign is also an exhibit on political campaigning in America."

Fenn, a staff assistant to JFK and a member of the U. S. Tariff Commission during his administration, also lectures at Harvard Business School where the favored teaching technique is the case study method. "Kennedy's life can be used as a case history to illustrate the political process," Fenn noted, "He was not a person to run away from the system—quite the contrary—he used a very political approach, used his charisma and position to enhance the business he was in."

That business, of course, was politics. JFK considered teaching and journalism after discharge from the Navy, both of which he had a flair for. (He covered the conference at which the United Nations was founded in 1945.) But, he had politics in his blood—and there was a vacancy in the eleventh Massachusetts Congressional District, a gerrymandered creation that incorporated some of Boston's most political ethnic neighborhoods. (Kennedy's predecessor was the legendary "Last Hurrah" mayor, James Michael Curley; he was followed by Thomas P. "Tip" O'Neill, Jr., who became speaker of the house.)

The young hero. Recovering from injuries received in the sinking of the PT-109 at Chelsea Naval Hospital near Boston, JFK was formally presented the Navy and Marine Corps Medal in June of 1944. He had already received the Purple Heart.

Dan H. Fenn, Jr., director of the Kennedy Library. A Boston native and a graduate of Harvard College, Fenn has been director of the JFK Library since 1971. He was named staff assistant to President Kennedy in 1961 and to the United States Tariff Commission in 1963, becoming vice chairman the following year. He teaches at Harvard Business School and has applied its famous "case study" method to the Kennedy Library's educational and outreach programs. A special concern is keeping the library a living institution: "We are rooted in the past, but not anchored in it."

(Photo: John Fitzgerald Kennedy Library)

There were nine other candidates for the seat and JFK was not favored to win. Photographs show a terribly thin, shy looking young man, but one who radiated sincerity. He was also a veteran, and a war hero. And, his family and friends campaigned hard in the neighborhoods for him.

Opponents charged that he was "a carpetbagger" with no real ties to the district. Powers recalled that he once shouted down a heckler by telling him: "When I was out in the Solomon Islands, nobody asked my address." He presented himself to the voters at rallies, on street corners and at house parties and was careful to note that: "My mother was born on Garden Court in the North End, my father on Webster Street in East Boston, my older brother, the late Joseph P. Kennedy, Jr., lived in Cambridge..."

This was still pre-television and JFK's campaign methods, as suggested by the posters, literature, and paraphernalia displayed were much like those of "Honey Fitz's" day. They still worked: JFK won a substantial victory. As the incumbent in a "safe" Democratic district, JFK was able to interest himself in national affairs taking liberal positions on social issues but favoring anti-Communist policies and a strong defense posture.

Much in demand as a speaker, and widely seen as a spokesman for his generation, as a congressman he addressed hundreds of groups in Massachusetts and was well known and liked from Cape Cod to the Berkshires. In 1952, he decided to run for the United States Senate seat held by Republican Henry Cabot Lodge, member of a distinguished Bay State family. (JFK's grandfather, "Honey Fitz", had run unsuccessfully against Lodge's grandfather for the U. S. Senate in 1916.)

Lodge was a respected senator and also a key figure in the Eisenhower presidential campaign. He was expected to ride in on "Ike's" coattails. JFK ran a hard campaign using an effective system of local coordinators directed by his campaign manager: Robert Kennedy. But, even more effective than the coordinators were the Kennedy women: his mother and sisters.

Among the exhibits is a silver tea service, of a type that occupies a legendary place in Massachusetts political history. Rose Kennedy and JFK's sisters gave tea party receptions all over the state to drum up support for him among women voters. Some seventy-five thousand women attended these teas: Kennedy defeated Lodge by seventy thousand, seven hundred and thirty-seven votes while Eisenhower was carrying Massachusetts by two hundred and eight thousand, eight hundred votes. Political observers concluded that Lodge had: "Drowned in seventy-five thousand cups of tea."

The fact that JFK had survived a massive Republican landslide made him a man to watch in the Democratic party. He took his oath with eleven other new Senate members including Barry Goldwater of Arizona, Mike Mansfield of Montana, and Stuart Symington of Missouri.

In 1954, while convalescing after a painful back operation, he began writing "Profiles in Courage," a study of political figures who stood by their principles in the face of pressure from their constituents. JFK's own popularity was at a low ebb in Massachusetts at the time because of his support of the St. Lawrence Seaway, which he thought was good for the country but many of his constituents thought was bad for the port of Boston. The book won the Pulitzer Prize, one of the honors he was proudest of.

Some of his notes for "Profiles" are displayed, scrawled on yellow legal pads. Much of the writing was done at night, when pain made it impossible for him to sleep.

In 1953, JFK married Jacqueline Bouvier, a New York and Newport, Rhode Island debutante who had been working as a photographer for the now defunct Washington Times Herald when they first met. The wedding reception was one of the social events of the year.

Rose Kennedy was to recall: "There were eight hundred in the church including

The young Congressman. Taken in 1947 when JFK was starting his first term in the United States House of Representatives but already recognized as one of the ablest of the wave of World War II veterans moving into politics.   (Photo: John Fitzgerald Kennedy Library)

The highly respected incumbent United States Senator Henry Cabot Lodge makes a point in a League of Women Voters debate in Waltham, Massachusetts, during the 1952 senatorial campaign. At first considered unbeatable, Lodge spent much of his time organizing Dwight D. Eisenhower's campaign for the Republican presidential nomination giving JFK an advantage he skillfully took advantage of.

(Photo: John Fitzgerald Kennedy Library)

Tea parties presided over by his mother and sisters proved to be a potent weapon in JFK's campaign arsenal in 1952. Held all over the state, they were attended by some seventy-five thousand women. Eisenhower carried Massachusetts by 208,800 votes, but JFK defeated Lodge by 70,737 votes. Eunice is shown modeling one of the skirts worn for these Kennedy Teas. Patricia and Mrs. Rose Kennedy are sitting, while JFK and Jean are standing behind the couch.

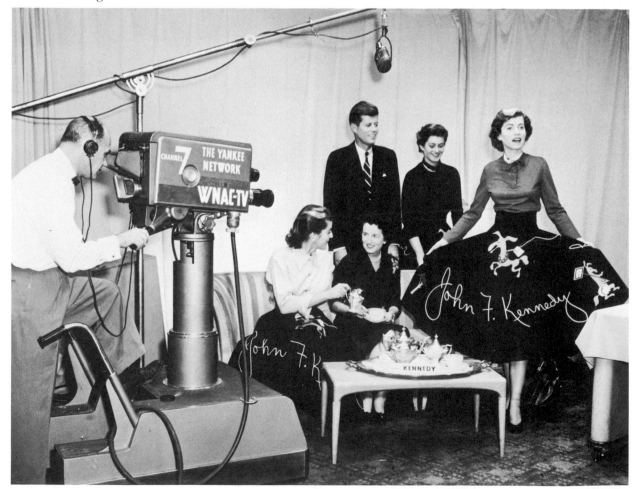

(Photo: John Fitzgerald Kennedy Library)

(Photo: John Fitzgerald Kennedy Library)

An unlikely trio. United States Senator John Kennedy, at right, greets a constituent: former heavy weight boxing champion Rocky Marciano, who had retired undefeated in 1956. Sports fan and then vice president Richard M. Nixon had his office in the Senate Office Building, a few doors down from JFK's.

all sorts of notables and more than twelve hundred at the reception... I daresay Jackie must have got a little tired of smiling and shaking hands, but I can't think of a more appropriate introduction to her new life as the wife of a political figure."

Wedding photographs show a handsome, smiling young couple, equally at home on the society page or the front page. But, it was after his marriage that JFK earned a reputation as a political heavy weight.

Adlai Stevenson was the favorite of Democratic liberals, including Kennedy, but not well liked by the old guard. In Massachusetts party traditionalists were led by veteran Congressman John McCormack. JFK challenged the old guard and was able to oust the old Democratic state chairman, a colorful but conservative pol called "Onions" Burke, and replace him with one of his own supporters, Mayor Lynch of Somerville—but only after a bare knuckles political fight.

JFK emerged with a reputation for clout as well as charm. He nominated Stevenson at the Democratic national convention in 1956 and came close to being the vice presidential candidate—an experience that made him determined to try for the presidential nomination at the next convention.

The 1960 campaign was one of the most significant in American history, and certainly one of the most dramatic. To many JFK symbolized the new generation: He was a child of the Twentieth Century, a decorated veteran of the war that was perhaps its most significant event. But, he faced an old obstacle: Religious prejudice.

New York's Alfred E. Smith, the Democratic candidate for president in 1928, was, like Kennedy, a Roman Catholic. Much of the opposition to his candidacy was on religious grounds and he was badly beaten by Republican Herbert Hoover, losing even traditionally Democratic southern states. It had become a political axiom that no Catholic could successfully seek the presidency. Anti-Catholic "hate" literature still circulated—some examples are exhibited—and polls indicated that a significant number of voters would not support a Catholic for president.

A television projector shows highlights of what was an enormously exciting campaign, as seemingly tireless JFK criss-crossed the country, pumping hands, addressing crowds, entering primaries. The religious issue wouldn't go away. When Hubert Humphrey, a mid-western Protestant, entered the primaries he was favored to carry West Virginia, considered a Bible Belt bastion. JFK campaigned largely on economic issues, won West Virginia handily—and clinched the nomination.

The religious issue still lingered, but was laid to rest in a dramatic meeting with the Protestant ministers of Houston, Texas at which Kennedy again declared his belief in the principle of separation of church and state. "I believe in an America where the separation of church and state is absolute." And then said:

"I believe in an America where religious intolerance will someday end... where there is no Catholic vote, no anti-Catholic vote, no bloc voting of any kind—and where Catholics, Protestants, and Jews will refrain from those attitudes of disdain and division which have so often marred their works in the past." The ministers were won over, and many of those close to JFK thought it the best speech he ever gave.

The real turning point of the campaign, however, was the first debate with Richard Nixon. Kennedy's cool confidence contrasted sharply on television screens with Nixon's clear anxiety, making JFK seem the one who was mature, experienced—and presidential. Even seen today in flickering, black and white television film by people who have no memory of the original event, the initial Kennedy-Nixon debate has the impact of raw history.

A very young Jacqueline Bouvier poses with a pet puppy in the 1930's.

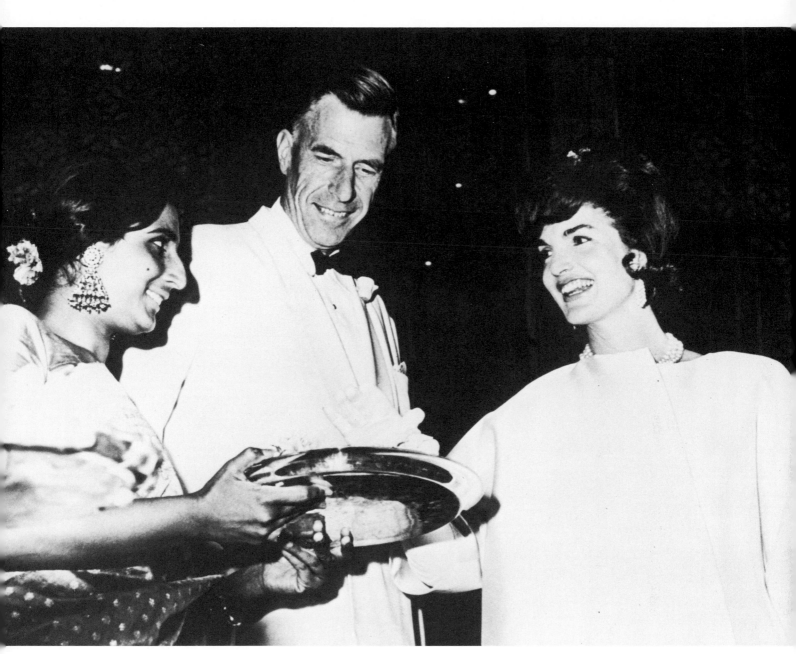

Jacqueline Kennedy accepts a welcoming gift of flowers from an Indian well-wisher as United States Ambassador Galbraith beams approvingly.

During a visit to India in March of 1962, Mrs. Jacqueline Kennedy frequently went for garden strolls with Prime Minister Pandit Nehru, who had personally invited her. In the background is his daughter Indira Gandhi, later herself Prime Minister of India, and United States Ambassador John Kenneth Galbraith.

"Ask not what your country can do for you..."   JFK making his inaugural speech on a cold January day in 1961.

There were two more debates—and Nixon performed better in them—but few voters were swayed by him. A few moments under the hot television lights made the crucial difference. The momentum had shifted to the Democrats, and to Kennedy.

Just how important the debate was became clear when the election returns came in. JFK had a clear majority in the Electoral College of three hundred and three to two hundred and nineteen but his popular vote margin was a slim one hundred and eighteen thousand, five hundred and fifty votes. John F. Kennedy had been elected the thirty-fifth president of the United States of America by the narrowest plurality in American history.

THE WHITE HOUSE YEARS

In popular memory, John F. Kennedy's term in the White House has become "A Thousand Days"—in good part because of Arthur Schlesinger's Pulitzer Prize winning biography of that title. In fact, it lasted over a month longer than that: A total of one thousand and thirty-seven days. Certainly a tragically short time for a youthful president to serve—at forty-three, JFK was the youngest man elected to the office, as well as the first Roman Catholic—but despite its brevity, the Kennedy administration was extraordinarily rich in achievements.

The Kennedy Library Museum uses five different exhibition areas to outline the highlights of JFK's "New Frontier" administration, along with some of the nuances and atmosphere of that "Camelot" era.

The Kennedy Administration:

"I said at the time of the Cuban disaster in April of 1961 that success has a hundred fathers and defeat is an orphan... the advice of those who were brought in on the executive branch was also unanimous, and the advice was wrong. And I was responsible." Thus, in 1962, did President Kennedy candidly admit his part in the Bay of Pigs disaster.

An attempt to overthrow the revolutionary government of Fidel Castro with American trained Cuban exiles, the Bay of Pigs invasion—named for the exile forces' landing spot on the southwest coast of Cuba—had been conceived by the Central Intelligence Agency (CIA) in 1960 and approved by President Eisenhower. JFK was briefed on the plan when he took office and allowed it to continue, insisting however that no American troops be used.

The Cuban exiles "assault brigade", consisting of fourteen hundred men, landed on April 16, 1961 and was almost immediately encircled by a strong pro-Castro force of twenty thousand troops supported by tanks, artillery and planes. The landing did not provoke a popular uprising against Castro, as had been hoped, and after three days of fighting the survivors of the invasion force were forced to surrender.

It was JFK's first major mistake, and historians generally agree the worst error of his administration. An angry President Kennedy set up a special committee, headed by General Maxwell Taylor to analyze what went wrong with what was officially called "Operation Zapata." He also negotiated a deal with Castro under which the prisoners were ransomed in 1962 for eleven million dollars worth of food, drugs, and medicine.

Among the exhibits is a vial of polio vaccine of the kind shipped to Cuba. Photographs show the Bay of Pigs and the Cuban exiles in action and also, being received by JFK after their release in a special ceremony at the Orange Bowl in Miami, where they presented him with one of their flags.

Cuba also provided the most dramatic—and dangerous—moment of the Kennedy administration: The Cuban Missile Crisis. The United States was aware that the Soviet Union was providing military aid to Cuba, but on October 16, 1962, President Kennedy was shown photographs that proved conclusively that the Russians were installing offensive missiles, capable of carrying nuclear warheads on the Caribbean island.

Missile bases in Cuba increased Soviet "first strike" capability against the United States by about fifty percent and made it

KASIMOV

(Photo: John Fitzgerald Kennedy Library)

KASIMOV
(CRATES BROKEN)

possible for Russian long-range missiles to hit almost every major American city while much of the east coast was within striking distance of medium-range Russian missiles. The continued presence of the rocket bases would clearly alter the world balance of power.

The Russians continued to insist that military aide to Cuba was purely defensive. But, at a tension-charged special meeting of the United Nations Security Council, United States ambassador Adlai Stevenson challenged the Soviet delegate to deny that there were Russian nuclear missiles in Cuba. "I am prepared to wait for my answer until hell freezes over." The sharp and detailed photographs taken by a U. S. airplane—some of which are in the exhibit—made the charge undeniable.

"This urgent transformation of Cuba into an important strategic base by the presence of these large, long-range and clearly offensive weapons of sudden mass destruction constitutes an explicit threat to the peace and security of all the Americas... a deliberately provocative and unjustified change in the

Airplane photographs, such as this one of the Soviet ship "Kasimov," showed crates of ballistic missiles stacked on the decks.

A photo taken by a United States airplane shows a Soviet vessel leaving Cuba in such detail, that the broken crates on the decks containing missiles are clearly visible. Aerial photos provided proof that Russia was constructing long-range missile installations that led to the Cuban Missile Crisis.

status quo which cannot be accepted by this country, if our courage and our commitments are ever to be trusted again by either friend or foe." President Kennedy had thrown down the gauntlet.

A surprise air attack on the bases was debated, but key advisors—led by Robert Kennedy—favored restraint. JFK demanded that Soviet leader Nikita Khrushchev remove the missiles and warned that a nuclear attack from Cuba on any nation in the Western Hemisphere would immediately trigger "a full retaliatory response" by the United States.

The United States imposed a naval blockade to prevent the installation of additional missiles. Soviet ships turned back to avoid a clash with the United States Navy, but work continued on the Cuban missile sites. JFK was reluctantly preparing for an invasion when Khrushchev made a conciliatory proposal: He would remove the missiles if the United States would agree not to invade Cuba. Kennedy accepted the offer and, although Khrushchev later tried to take a tougher stance, the crisis abated and the way was paved for detente.

The true significance of the Cuban Missile Crisis is still a matter of debate, and some aspects of it remain shrouded in secrecy, but it certainly had brought the United States closer to a world war than at any time since World War II. JFK was aware of the historical importance—and the dangers—of the events of October, 1962. Later, as a memento to those who were at his side then, he gave "Cuban Missile Crisis" calenders with those thirteen memorable days outlined. The one displayed in the library museum belonged to Jacqueline Kennedy. JFK was outwardly calm in these crises but expressed some of his inner feelings by doodling on yellow legal pads. (Discussing the Bay of Pigs, he misspelled "decesions" seventeen times.)

Although not as severe, an earlier crisis over Berlin also had provoked fears of war and turned into a test of wills between Kennedy and Khrushchev. At a summit meeting in Vienna in June of 1961, the Soviet leader threatened to make a separate peace treaty with East Germany, ending the "occupation" status under which the United States and other western troops remained in West Berlin. He said he would sign the treaty in December of 1961, after which western forces would have to leave the city.

"We cannot and will not permit the Communists to drive us out of Berlin, either gradually or by force," Kennedy declared. He refused to back down, called military reservists back to active duty, and asked Congress to increase the defense budget.

One of the main reasons the Russians wanted the west out of Berlin was to prevent East Germans from fleeing their Communist regime, as thousands did annually. In August of 1961 the Berlin Wall went up, effectively stopping the flow of refugees and in October Khrushchev postponed the East German treaty deadline—a virtual admission that Kennedy had outbluffed him.

During the crisis, JFK sent additional troops to Berlin as a gesture of support and to emphasize United States' right to have access to the city. In June of 1963, he went there himself. Speaking to a large and enthusiastic crowd just a few yards from the Berlin Wall, he declared: "Ich bin ein Berliner"—"I am a Berliner."

Among the photos and documents in the Berlin crisis exhibit is the draft of that famous speech, along with the carefully edited text of the one he delivered to the nation on the subject.

But, besides dealing with crises, the Kennedy administration met some challenges and moved the country in some new directions. One was to step up the Space Program by sending Astronaut John Glenn into orbit in a manned space craft. This decision was opposed by some science advisors, who felt the project was risky and had little scientific value since the Soviet cosmonauts had already demonstrated that man could withstand weightlessness.

JFK approved the flight, a decision often cited as an example of his skillful use of the dramatic gesture to promote policies he advocated. Colonel Glenn's successful flight caught the imagination of the nation and moved the nation a giant step towards its avowed goal of landing a man on the moon before 1970.

Kennedy was impressed by the courage of the astronauts, they in turn found him supportive and sympathetic. JFK valued the model of Glenn's Friendship VII, along with other rocket and spacecraft models presented to him. Exhibited with these, somewhat poignantly is a three billion year-old fragment of moon rock brought back to earth by the Apollo 15 mission in 1971. JFK did not live to see it, but the goal he set for America was reached on July 20, 1969 when Neil A. Armstrong became the first man to set foot on the moon.

As a living example of youth in action, President Kennedy had a particular rapport with young people and they were among his most enthusiastic supporters—around the world. One of the New Frontier's most successful and imaginative innovations was the Peace Corps. Although not limited solely to young people, the Peace Corps—composed of volunteers who worked on education, public health and economic development projects in Third World countries—appealed particularly to the idealism and sense of adventure of young Americans.

As one Peace Corps volunteer put it in 1962: "I've never done anything political, patriotic or unselfish because nobody ever asked me to. Kennedy asked." In later years, an older volunteer was to write from India: "...I didn't dream that in this remote corner of the world—so far away from the people and material things that I always considered so necessary, I discover what life is really all about." That was written by Mrs. Lillian Carter, mother of President Jimmy Carter, in 1968.

"Ich bin ein Berliner." JFK's emotion charged visit to West Berlin, where he was enthusiastically received, was highlighted by his declaration that: "I am a Berliner."

(Photo: John Fitzgerald Kennedy Library)

During his visit to West Berlin in June of 1963, President Kennedy inspected the Berlin Wall and the Brandenburg Gate, symbol of the divided city.

One effect of the Cuban revolution was a new awareness of Latin America and its problems among Americans. To prevent the spread of Castroism, Kennedy conceived the Alliance for Progress. The alliance, JFK said, would: "Demonstrate to the entire world that man's unsatisfied aspiration for economic progress and social justice can best be achieved by free men working within a framework of democratic institutions."

Even Fidel Castro said of the alliance that it was: "A politically wise concept... a very intelligent concept."

Economic progress at home was also a Kennedy concern. He used a mix of economic tools such as a thirteen billion dollar tax reduction to stimulate consumer spending, programs for those too poor to pay taxes, tax credits to encourage business investment, and "guideposts" to restrain price and wage increases. The formula worked well, giving the United States one of its longest peacetime periods of non-inflationary economic growth. When steel companies tried to ignore the guidelines and raise prices, JFK ordered the federal government to stop doing business with them and urged Americans to boycott them.

Steel prices were rolled back—and his image as a leader considerably enhanced. Polls taken that year, 1962, indicated that fifty-eight percent of the American people favored Kennedy's actions on steel prices and fifty-six percent of them thought their standard of living was going up.

But, the most urgent domestic issues confronting the Kennedy administration were racial justice and civil rights for black Americans. Videotapes of "freedom rides" and civil rights demonstrations convey the turmoil and tension of a period that saw blacks launch a massive assault on segregation, one that often provoked a violent response.

Attorney General Robert Kennedy dispatched United States marshals, who became an elite corps of federal law enforcement officers during the Kennedy administration, to protect travelers on interstate buses and to protect a black veteran, James Meredith whose efforts to attend classes at the University of Mississippi provoked riots in which two people were killed, dozens injured. Meredith completed his studies at "Old Miss," graduating in 1963. Racial segregation at southern state universities soon ended.

In June of 1963, federal officials escorted black students seeking to register at the Universtiy of Alabama. Governor George Wallace, who had vowed to "stand in the schoolhouse door" to prevent integration of of Alabama schools, stepped aside after a token protest.

That United States marshals had to cope with physical violence to enforce the law is attested to by one of the museum exhibits: A rock-battered steel helmet worn by a federal marshal in a civil rights demonstration.

The highwater mark of the Civil Rights movement was August 1963 when more than two hundred thousand people marched on Washington, D. C. calling for freedom and jobs and heard Reverend Martin Luther King eloquently say: "I have a dream that... we will be able to speed up that day when all of God's children, black men, and white men, Jews and gentiles, Protestants and Catholics, will be able to join hands and sing, in the words of the old Negro spiritual, 'Free at last, free at last. Thank God Almighty, we are free at last.'"

In June of 1963, JFK had sent a comprehensive civil rights bill, covering voting, public accomodations, education, and employment to Congress—which was still considering it when he was assassinated. At the urging of President Lyndon Johnson, who told Congress that nothing "could more eloquently honor President Kennedy's memory than the... civil rights bill for which he fought so long," it became law in 1964, seven months after Kennedy's death. A copy is displayed.

The Kennedy family had final approval of all exhibits in the museum, and was particularly interested in the exhibit devoted to mental retardation, a special concern of President Kennedy's and a continuing one of his family.

Most visitors to the library are brought up short as they enter the exhibits by a large photo mural of all eleven Kennedys—Joseph, Rose, and their nine children—taken in London on the eve of World War II. All are smiling and look happy and healthy. One of the commonest questions museum guides are asked is: "But, which one is retarded?" The answer is Rosemary, the pretty girl third from left, with her arm around her brother John.

"Although retarded children may be the victims of fate, they will not be the victims of our neglect," JFK said in 1963. He had initiated legislation to stimulate research into the causes and prevention of mental retardation and to improve the care of the mentally retarded and increase the number of trained professionals working with them.

"I often ask myself: 'Why did my brother act? Why was he concerned? Was it only because we had a mentally retarded sister?' I think not. I think he asked himself deep and troubling questions about human value. How do we measure human worth. How do we distribute our national resources. How do we decide who is worthy to receive medical care? And I believe he asked himself the most difficult question of all: What are our duties to the powerless if we are to be a caring, just and family-oriented society?"

So spoke Eunice Kennedy Shriver, who served as a consultant to the president's panel on mental retardation, and was formally presented with a pen used by JFK to sign a new mental retardation act.

On November 21, 1963—the day before he died—President Kennedy asked Congress for forty-three million dollars to carry out the new mental retardation programs. The funds were quickly appropriated.

One of the goals of the New Frontier was a reduction of armaments and a particular concern of the 1960's was the spread of radioactive fallout from nuclear tests in the atmosphere. In the spring of 1963, he delivered a major address on what he called "the most important topic on earth: world peace." Both the United States and the

Soviet Union, he said, were "caught up in a vicious and dangerous cycle in which suspicion on one side breeds suspicion on the other and new weapons begat counter weapons." In the nuclear age, he concluded, peace became "the necessary rational end of rational men." Determined to break the cycle, he proposed a treaty.

Averell Harriman, who had been Franklin Roosevelt's ambassador to Moscow, was picked by JFK as chief United States negotiator for the Nuclear Test Ban Treaty, a job calling for both restraint and toughness. On October 7, 1963, President Kennedy signed the documents ratifying the treaty—one of the major accomplishments of his administration "...a shaft of light cut into the darkness."

THE PRESIDENT AND THE PRESS

Few presidents have been as comfortable with the press as John Kennedy. As he was fond of pointing out, he had been a reporter himself covering the founding conference of the United Nations and the British elections in 1945—his battered old typewriter is displayed—and felt a kindred feeling for journalists.

And, no president before or since held press conferences as often. During his three years in office, JFK had sixty-four White House news conferences—averaging one every sixteen days. He was the first president to permit his press conferences to be televised live, an innovation that proved extremely popular: It's estimated that they had an audience of nearly sixty-five million viewers around the world.

Noisy, lively, and full of a sense of the immediate and the unexpected, these news conferences had enormous impact especially overseas where their candor and informality caused a sensation.

The President and the Press exhibit consists of selected videotaped excerpts from White House press conferences, with emphasis on Kennedy's humor, decisiveness, grace, and rapport with the press. It is still a lively show, and the Kennedy personality—and

50

charisma—comes across strongly: Gracefully fielding questions amid urgent shouts of "Mr. President!" "Mr. President!"; joking with a female reporter; defending a new tariff, "It's going to stand,"; admitting forthrightly that it was unfair to call up some reservists during the Berlin crisis, but not others, "...life is unfair."

Museum goers are fascinated, those old enough to remember the original, live conferences usually nostalgic as well.

PERSONAL INTERESTS, CULTURAL AFFAIRS, AND FAMILY LIFE

The Kennedy White House was a very lively place. The youth of the presidential family and the wide ranging personal interests of President and Mrs. Kennedy caused it to be the scene of glittering social and cultural events as well as routine state functions. And, always, it was the headquarters of the active and vigorous Kennedy clan.

There is an audio track in this exhibit area, but the choice of music is not random: It is famed cellist Pablo Casals, recorded live at a White House concert. Casals, a political exile from Spain had refused to perform in countries that recognized the Franco government, but made an exception for Kennedy, performing at a special concert in the executive mansion on November 13, 1961.

Cultural events of this kind, as well as the frequent presence of writers and performing artists on social occasions contributed much to the special atmosphere of the White House during the Kennedy years.

Exhibits cover such things as youth programs and concerts, the restoration of the White House which Jacqueline Kennedy supervised, and festivities surrounding the inaugural. (The President and Mrs. Kennedy attended five inaugural balls.) Among the items displayed are gowns worn by Jacqueline and Rose Kennedy—the latter wore the same gown to her son's inaugural ball she had to the Court of St. James when her husband presented his credentials as United States ambassador to Britain.

Photographs, letters, some of his favorite books, paintings, and ship models, drawings by his daughter Caroline, and other personal mementoes illustrate different facets of JFK and aspects of life in his extraordinarily close and spirited family. "All the Kennedys," newspaper columnist Joseph Alsop said, "are in love with each other." As the exhibit makes clear, the bonds of family were strengthened by frequent reunions and meetings and constant communication by telephone, telegraph, and mail.

In his official capacity, President Kennedy both gave and received gifts. When presenting gifts to heads of state, a special effort was made to find objects that both represented the United States and would have meaning to the recipient. A letter from George Washington to Lafayette's brother-in-law, the Vicomte de Noailles went to President de Gaulle of France, for instance, while President de Valera of Ireland received a Civil War battle flag of the sixty-ninth New York Regiment—the famous "Fighting Irish."

In 1963, President Kennedy commissioned a retired craftsman from the arsenal in Rock Island, Illinois to reproduce the silver mounted sword that Washington carried in battle during the American revolution. The first reproduction went to Emperor Haile Selassie of Ethiopia, another is exhibited.

Visiting dignitaries were often as adroit at selecting official gifts that were both suitable and symbolic as JFK himself. On behalf of the Irish people, Prime Minister Sean Lemass presented a Fourteenth Century treaty between the Earl of Ormonde and "John O'Kenedy (sic) and those of his nation." In 1963, King Hassan II gave President Kennedy a copy of the new Moroccan constitution. In 1789, Washington had made a similar presentation of the then new American constitution to Emperor Mohammed I of Morocco.

Unlike other presidential libraries, the Kennedy has nothing in it selected specifically for the library by President Kennedy himself. That had to be done by others. A particular interest of Curator David F. Powers, who knew JFK intimately, were the various gifts and presents sent to the president by admiring citizens. They include a replica of an American flag made of two thousand and thirty-seven small pieces of wood screwed and glued together by a sixty-nine year old Portugese immigrant, Joseph Dias; a four hundred year old map of Ireland; a piece of whalebone scrimshaw; remnants of a flag attributed to Betsy Ross; a realistic marine scene by a Canadian artist.

Few American presidents have been as concerned about raising the standards of American cultural life as President Kennedy, or thought the arts so important. The national cultural center which he advocated, became the Kennedy Center—a model is on display in the museum—and among the several JFK quotes inscribed on it is this one:

"There is a connection, hard to explain logically but easy to feel, between achievement in public life and progress in the arts. The age of Pericles was also the age of Phidias. The age of Elizabeth also the age of Shakespeare. And the New Frontier for which I campaign in public life, can also be a new frontier for American art."

Pakistan's President Ayub Khan was greeted personally by President Kennedy when he arrived for a state visit. He is shown leaving Andrews Air Force Base in the presidential limousine after reviewing a guard of honor.

JFK at a White House press conference.

President and Madame Bourguiba with President and Mrs. Kennedy before White House state dinner. Tunisia's President Habib Bourguiba was a White House guest in the spring of 1961. Bourguiba was a supporter of United States policies in North Africa and was admired by JFK.

(Photo: John Fitzgerald Kennedy Library)

Back in the White House. Former President Harry S. Truman and wife Bess were guests of honor at a White House state dinner in 1961. The Truman's daughter Margaret is in the background with husband Clifton Daniels, a New York Times editor.

(Photo: John Fitzgerald Kennedy Library)

Mental retardation was a problem of particular concern to JFK, whose sister Rosemary was so afflicted and he initiated legislation to step up research into the causes of mental retardation and to improve the treatment of those suffering from it. In this photo, he is shown signing the bill into law. On November 21, 1963, the day before he died, he asked Congress for $43 million to implement the new programs.

The three brothers. This smiling photo of Robert, Edward and John Kennedy was taken in the Oval Office of the White House on August 28, 1963.

(Photo: John Fitzgerald Kennedy Library)

(Photo: John Fitzgerald Kennedy Library)

JFK, John John, and Caroline hold the reins of the children's pet pony outside the entrance of the Oval Office. His children's casual access to the presidential inner sanctum sometimes startled visitors but delighted press and public.

While Daddy claps, Caroline and John F. Kennedy, Jr. dance around the presidential seal woven into the Oval Office carpet. (Photo: *John Fitzgerald Kennedy Library*)

Caroline Kennedy and a young friend play hide and seek inside the president's desk, a gift to the White House from Queen Victoria—who might not have approved.

While President Kennedy apparently ponders affairs of state, daughter Caroline plays with his bookends: modeled after the cannon on the USS Constitution, first ship of the United States Navy. (Photo: John Fitzgerald Kennedy Library)

(Photo: John Fitzgerald Kennedy Library)

A sailor president. JFK loved to sail and did so as often as he could while president. Here he is shown at the wheel of the United States Coast Guard yacht "Manitou," off Newport, where he was married and a favorite summer vacation spot.

John Kennedy, Jr. gets a warming hug from his father on a brisk September day, while exploring a beached dory at Newport, Rhode Island. The Kennedys often went to Newport, usually staying at Hammersmith Farm, the palatial shingled residence of Jacqueline's relations, the Auchinclosses. *(Photo: John Fitzgerald Kennedy Library)*

A DAY IN THE LIFE OF THE PRESIDENT

What does a president do all day? Small children often ask that question on tours of the White House. The answer, of course, depends on the president but in modern times American heads of state have been kept very busy, indeed.

Just how busy is illustrated by one day of JFK's administration—one of the longest, it should be said—September 25, 1962.

It began at 7:15 a.m., when JFK awoke and read the papers and ended at 2:45 a.m. the following morning with the president and Mrs. Kennedy returning home after a British embassy party.

Using a sophisticated audiovisual technique in which slide photos dissolve into each other, the exhibit lets the stream of visitors and appointments JFK dealt with flood over the viewer. Among other things that day, he conferred with his security advisors, accepted the credentials of foreign diplomats, had a reunion with survivors of the PT-109, greeted a ballet troupe, watched a boxing match, and went to the theater.

Life was once more leisurely for an American president. Display cases exhibit diaries and appointment books of other presidents, from the beginning of the republic until the present: Washington, Adams, Polk, Lincoln, Wilson, Roosevelt, Eisenhower, Kennedy, and Carter. A look at them suggests that United States presidents were not really overworked—at least until this century.

On July 1, 1790, for example, George Washington's diary reveals that he went horseback riding for exercise from 5 to 7 a.m., discussed foreign affairs with his vice president during the day, and had dinner with the secretaries of state, war, and treasury (with their ladies) at night. That was all. Of course, at that time the United States had a population of only 3.9 million, an area of 888, 811 square miles and a federal budget of $3.6 million.

By the time JFK took office, the country had a population of 183.7 million, encompassed 3.6 million square miles, the federal budget was $90.3 billion, and the presidency a full time job—and then some.

JFK greeted Mexico's famous Ballet Folklorico at the White House on September 25, 1962. He is shown here, on the steps of the portico, speaking to members of the troupe.

(Photo: John Fitzgerald Kennedy Library)

Accepting painting "The Whites of Their Eyes," which depicts the Battle of Bunker Hill in Charlestown, Massachusetts, JFK meets former constituents from his old congressional district. United States Representative Thomas P. "Tip" O'Neil, who succeeded him as congressman, is to the left of the president.   (Photo: John Fitzgerald Kennedy Library)

(Photo: John Fitzgerald Kennedy Library)

One of the many groups JFK spoke to on September 25 was an organization of Congressional aides, assistants to congressmen and senators, who receive little publicity but play an important part in the legislative process.

On that very long day of September 25, 1962, President Kennedy also added to his cabinet. Here, he stands by a newly sworn in Secretary of Labor Willard Wirtz.

One of JFK's most dramatic early decisions was to authorize Astronaut Alan Shepard's flight into space in the wake of Russian cosmonaut Yuri Gagarin's successful one, the first in history. Some advisors thought the flight dangerous and unnecessary but President Kennedy felt it would catch the imagination of the country and signal the world that the United States did not intend to be left behind in the space race. The flight was a success: Shepard orbited one hundred and fifteen miles into the upper atmosphere and returned unharmed. Here, JFK and Mrs. Kennedy are shown watching the space shot on a White House TV set. Then Vice President Lyndon Johnson is at left.

(Photo: John Fitzgerald Kennedy Library)

At Eleanor Roosevelt's funeral in November, 1962, President Kennedy stood among the mourners with former presidents Harry S. Truman and Dwight D. Eisenhower, providing a rare photo of three United States presidents together. (Photo: John Fitzgerald Kennedy Library)

President Kennedy presiding over a cabinet meeting in the White House. Adlai Stevenson, United States Ambassador to the United Nations, is second from left; Lyndon Johnson—then vice president—is third from left. (Photo: John Fitzgerald Kennedy Library)

An enthusiastic crowd in Billings, Montana, presses forward to greet President Kennedy during his "conservation tour" in the fall of 1963. One father lifted his son over his head to enable him to shake JFK's hand. (Photo: John Fitzgerald Kennedy Library)

President Kennedy making some introductory remarks at the opening of the Mona Lisa exhibition at the National Gallery in January, 1963. Seated from left are Mrs. Andre Malraux; Mrs. Kennedy; Malraux, noted author and French minister of culture; and Secretary of State Dean Rusk.

At a dinner in the White House in April, 1962, for Nobel Prize winners, JFK chats with novelist Pearl Buck while Mrs. Kennedy speaks to poet Robert Frost. Lady Bird Johnson is at left.

President and Mrs. Kennedy being greeted upon arrival at Dallas Airport on November 22, 1963. Moments later, their motorcade departed for the city.

THE OFFICE OF THE PRESIDENT

The exhibit devoted to the office of the president is almost literally that: A replica of the main feature of Kennedy's office in the Oval Office of the White House—his desk.

It is a piece of furniture with a very rich history. In 1854 a British naval vessel on an Arctic expedition, H.M.S. Resolute was abandoned by its crew. But, the following year the ship was salvaged by an American whaler and returned to Queen Victoria as a gift from the American people. When the Resolute was scrapped in 1878, Queen Victoria had a desk made from its timbers and presented to United States President Rutherford B. Hayes.

The desk had been in storage for many years when Mrs. Kennedy came upon it, and knowing how much her husband loved both history and the sea, restored it to the Oval Office. The desk remained in the White House after Kennedy's death and, when the Kennedy library opened its doors in 1979, was being used by President Carter.

What the museum displays is an artful copy, authentic looking in every respect from its ornate carving to the worn brass commemorative plaque with an inscription in spidery victorian.

The contents of the desk are authentic, however, and it has been arranged exactly as it was when JFK left for Dallas on November 21, 1963. The black alligator desk set was a gift from President Charles de Gaulle of France, on the memo pad are notes on the nuclear test ban treaty and world peace scribbled by JFK. Books, including a copy of "Profiles in Courage," are kept in place by book ends modeled on the guns of the USS Constitution and made for President Kennedy by a retired naval officer.

Among the other objects on the desk are three telephones, one with an open line to all staff members; a wooden ink holder and double pen sets for signing official documents; an initialed lighter and ashtrays, one embedded with fingerprints, a gift of FBI director J. Edgar Hoover.

There are three chairs, all with special significance to JFK. Two are wooden captain's chairs, one presented by the 1964 freshman class at Harvard College, the other a gift from the Choate alumni in 1961. Kennedy's rocking chair became something of a symbol of his unstuffy presidential style, but he used it for strictly practical reasons: It relieved the back pains resulting from his old war injury. The chair itself, a bentwood rocker from North Carolina, was given to him by his father. The cushions were gifts of the Navy, presented at a fleet review in 1963. (Among the more popular items in the Kennedy Library gift shop is a kit for those who want to hook replicas.)

Among the personal momentoes left behind are a gold inaugural medal, a Waterford crystal ashtray with the Kennedy coat of arms, a Steuben glass sculpture with an etching of the PT-109, a gift of Navy PT boat veterans of the Pacific; a piece of scrimshaw, and photographs of his children, Caroline and John Jr.

In the center of the desk, mounted on wood, is the coconut on which Lieutenant Kennedy carved the message: "Commander/Native Knows Posit/He Can Pilot/11 Alive/Need Small Boat/Kennedy." Carried to an Australian coastwatcher on Kolombangara Island in the Solomons, this message led to the rescue of the crew of the PT-109. For curator Powers, this is the most valuable item in the museum. "It's got to be," he said, "it saved his life."

"For only the president represents the national interest and upon him alone converge all the needs and aspirations of all parts of the country, all departments of the government, all nations of the world," Kennedy said in a 1962 speech.

Around the walls of the circular presidential office exhibit are twelve windows, each displaying documents and JFK quotations illustrating a different presidential function: Conducting foreign policy, serving as commander in chief of the armed forces, acting as head of his political party, and so forth. The intended effect is that of a diagram showing that the president is at the center of a wheel of power, within which there are other interrelated wheels of power.

ROBERT F. KENNEDY

The lives of John and Robert Kennedy were inextricably intertwined. RFK was his brother's campaign manager, political advisor and confidant. As attorney general, he was responsible for implementing New Frontier policy, particularly in key areas such as civil rights. As a United States Senator from New York he continued to champion causes associated with President Kennedy, and at the time of his death in 1968 was running for president, pledged to continue the policies of his brother. "I do not run for the presidency to oppose any man... I run to seek new policies—to close the gaps between black and white, rich and poor, young and old, in this country and around the world."

Robert Francis Kennedy was born on November 20, 1925, the seventh of the nine Kennedy children and the smallest of the boys, a physical fact which in the competitive atmosphere of the Kennedy family made him determined to keep up with his older brothers. He went to seven different schools in ten years, finishing high school at a Massachusetts preparatory school, Milton Academy, in 1944. After serving in the naval reserve and as an apprentice seaman on the destroyer USS Joseph P. Kennedy Jr., he returned to Harvard with the class of 1948.

In June of 1950, while a law student at the University of Virginia, he married Ethel Skakel. They were to have eleven children and their exuberant and energetic life style at Hickory Hill—a handsome antebellum mansion in McLean, Virginia, just outside Washington, D.C.—was much admired.

RFK's entire working career was in public service, beginning in the Justice Department, which he was later to head as attorney general. In 1953, he spent six months on the staff of the McCarthy Committee—headed by the controversial Senator Joseph McCarthy—but resigned because of disagreement over the course the committee was taking.

After working for the Hoover Commission, he rejoined the Senate investigations committee and became chief counsel in 1955, directing probes of waste and graft in federal agencies.

In 1957, the Senate created a select committee to investigate labor racketeering. RFK was chief counsel for the committee and directed one of the most extensive congressional investigations ever undertaken. More than three hundred days of public hearings were held and some fifteen hundred witnesses questioned. The investigation led to shakeups in several unions, particularly the Teamsters Union—a particular target of the probe—and major legislation reforming the way unions were run was passed.

Named attorney general at the age of thirty-five, he was one of the youngest men ever to hold that position. Initially, his credentials were questioned by many—especially liberals who remembered the McCarthy connection—and some thought him too young and inexperienced. But, he proved a vigorous and effective attorney general and for the first time the Justice Department wholeheartedly supported the legal rights of black Americans: Five hundred and fifty federal law enforcement officers were sent to the University of Mississippi to protect James Meredith and safeguard his right to enroll.

The exhibit includes a chronology of significant events during his time in office, from the first coordinated federal investigation of organized crime begun on January 23, 1961—three days after he took office—to September, 1964 when he resigned to run for the Senate.

Although attacked as a "carpetbagger" he campaigned hard and, aided by a Lyndon Johnson landslide nationally, carried New York by 719,693 votes.

As a senator, he identified himself with the cause of disadvantaged groups such as migrant farm workers, the rural poor, and the ghetto dwellers of large cities. He made a speech or issued a statement to the press on the average of every two days, the subjects ranging from river pollution to nuclear weapons.

In 1968, Senator Eugene McCarthy's strong showing in the New Hampshire primary demonstrated the depth of the anti-Viet Nam War feeling in the Democratic party. Originally favoring United States involvement, RFK came to believe that the war was a mistake: "I was involved in many of the early decisions on Viet Nam, decisions which helped set us on our present path... I am willing to bear my share of responsibility before history and before my fellow citizens. But past error is no excuse for its own perpetuation. Tragedy is a tool for the living to gain wisdom, not a guide by which to live."

His presidential candidacy was not enthusiastically received by party leaders, but public support appeared strong. On March 31, 1968, President Johnson unexpectedly announced that he would not be a candidate for reelection. RFK won primaries in Indiana, Nebraska, and the District of Columbia. He lost to McCarthy in Oregon, but went on to win in South Dakota and most important of all, California on June 4. He was shot at a victory party in Los Angeles on June 5, and died the following day.

Through photographs, documents, momentoes, and memorabilia, the exhibit tries to portray this vigorous, intense, and complicated man. They include such things as his Harvard letter sweater, his law degree—the first professional degree earned by a member of the Kennedy family, and the ice axe he used to climb Mount Kennedy.

The latter is a Canadian mountain, and at the time it was named for John F. Kennedy (1964), it was the tallest unclimbed peak in North America. Though no mountaineer, and not fond of heights, RFK scaled the fourteen thousand foot mountain in company with two veterans of the successful 1963 Everest expedition. "I climbed this remote but spectacularly beautiful mountain because it was named after President Kennedy. It is nothing more complicated than that."

The style and personality of Robert Kennedy was subject of a moving documentary by Charles Guggenheim, "RFK Remembered," which was shown at the 1968 Democratic convention and over all television networks to an audience of millions. Excerpts from the prize winning film are shown on videotape in the last exhibit area of the museum.

The Kennedy Library deals with the lives of John and Robert Kennedy not their deaths, or the circumstances surrounding them. Visitors often ask to see the exhibits on the two assassinations, but there are none. The John F. Kennedy time line ends with the notation that the Apollo lunar capsule had completed its first launching test. The last exhibit is a photograph of the President and Mrs. Kennedy, both looking relaxed and smiling happily, taken at the Dallas airport just before they boarded the motorcade that would take them through the city. Next to it is a plain red oak panel and the inscription: "On November 22, 1963 John Fitzgerald Kennedy was assassinated in Dallas, Texas." A similar panel ends the Robert Kennedy exhibit.

Visitors exit the museum to the taped sounds of New England that JFK loved: the crash of the ocean, the wind, and the cry of sea birds. Before them is a great glass window out of which they can see Dorchester Bay and beyond the entrance to Boston Harbor: Presidents Roads.

The transition from the constraining corridors and subdued lighting of the museum to the brightness and vast space of the glass pavilion of the library is startling, and was meant to be.

Architect I. M. Pei conceived the ten-story room as a place where people could think about what they had seen, and let those thoughts soar. It's safe to say that many also carry those thoughts with them when they leave.

At the precise center of the Kennedy Library building, and the focal point around which the exhibition area revolves, is an exact replica of the antique desk that stood in the Oval Office of the JFK White House. All items on the desk are authentic and are exactly as they were when President Kennedy departed for Dallas on November 21, 1963.

The Archives

When George Washington moved back to Mount Vernon in 1797 he brought home his accumulated records, a precedent followed by the next thirty-one presidents. The fact is that up until 1978 a president did not have to surrender any—let alone all—of his papers to the public. If Richard Nixon had not argued personal ownership and presidential constitutional privilege to deny investigators access to his records, the question of who ultimately owns presidential documents might still be hotly debated, as it was for more than a century.

A general feeling that presidential papers should be preserved and studied is documented by the hundreds of thousands of dollars appropriated by Congress during the nineteenth century to collect the papers of Washington, Jefferson, Madison, Monroe and Jackson. When a Manuscript Division was established within the Library of Congress in 1897 these papers were deposited in it. By the time Calvin Coolidge left office in 1928 many of the records of twenty-three predecessors had been salvaged.

Andrew Jackson's papers had, however, been lost when the Hermitage burned in 1834. The papers of William Harrison and John Tyler had also been burned and those belonging to Presidents Pierce, Grant, Van Buren, Fillmore and Harding had been screened and extensively destroyed. Chester Arthur's papers had simply vanished.

It was Franklin Roosevelt who conceived the idea of a distinct, federally maintained library to house his papers. In 1938 Roosevelt spoke to a group of historians about his plan to stow "what might be called a source material collection relating to a specific period in our history... in a modern, fireproof building... so designed that it would hold all my own collection and also such other material relating to this period... as might be donated... in the future by other members of the administration."

This building was to be at Hyde Park, Roosevelt's estate on the Hudson near New York City. He reasoned that scattering libraries such as this around the country would stimulate local study of the presidency and help to preserve its records in case of bombing. In 1939 a joint resolution of Congress authorized the Archivist of the United States (the Archives themselves had just been instituted in 1934) to accept and maintain this particular president's papers, library building and land.

If this prototype had failed that might have been the end of presidential libraries. But it was—and continues to be—an unquestionably useful place. In March, 1950, when Roosevelt's papers were formally opened to the public, fifty-eight percent of them were available to researchers. Will Johnson, archivist in charge of research at the Kennedy Library, points out: "This was only a few months after the opening of the balance of the Lincoln papers at the Library of Congress and several years before the opening of the papers of the two Adams presidents."

Be it said that a few widely scattered libraries already housed some presidential papers: Rutherford Hayes' papers are in a Hayes Memorial Library built by the State of Ohio in 1914, Hoover's papers had been deposited at Stanford University and a small collection of Coolidge memorabilia and papers can be seen in the Forbes Library, Northampton, Massachusetts.

Roosevelt's idea of a Federally maintained institution—designed both to serve serious scholars and to educate the public was, however, entirely new and all-American. (No other head of state had ever proposed opening his records to public scrutiny.) The idea caught on.

In 1955 a Presidential Libraries Act formalized the nation's willingness "to accept for deposit... the papers and other historical materials of any president or former president of the United States, or of any other official in the government," also "other papers relating to and contemporary with any President or former President of the United States" along with "any land, buildings and equipment offered as a gift to the United States for the purpose of creating a presidential archival depository... and to maintain, operate and protect them as presidential archival property."

There are now six more presidential libraries: Truman's in Independence, Missouri (1957), Eisenhower's in Abilene, Kansas (1962), Hoover's in West Branch, Iowa (also opened in 1962, incorporating most of the material still duplicated at Stanford), Johnson's in Austin, Texas (1971) and Ford's—its library in Ann Arbor, its museum in Grand Rapids. The Kennedy Library's archives were first opened to researchers in 1969; their final quarters and museum came a decade later.

Like Roosevelt, JFK was himself a historian, keenly aware that: "Documents are the primary sources of history; they are the means by which later generations draw close to historical events and enter into the thoughts, fears and hopes of the past."

Five days after his inauguration Kennedy had his pre-presidential papers—some eight hundred and sixty thousand pages, principally documents from his campaign, congressional and senatorial files—transferred to the National Archives. In 1961 he announced his plans for placing his presidential library at Harvard University in Cambridge, Massachusetts. The following May, Arthur Schlesinger, the administration's historian in residence, sent a letter to key officials, asking them to preserve their own personal as well as official files for eventual deposit in the Library.

Within two weeks of the president's death the John Fitzgerald Kennedy Library Corporation was born. The responsibility for organizing the presidential papers and memorabilia was immediately assumed by the National Archives. And within a month the oral history project, the most ambitious series of interviews ever conducted about a former head of state, was launched.

It was in August, 1966, that the first shipment of the records of John F. Kennedy and his associates was trucked from Washington to a new Federal Records Center in Waltham, Massachusetts. This out-of-the-way warehouse is a limbo for billions of Federal documents—old tax records and the like—which have been retired and are in the process of being reduced to that one percent which will be preserved in the National Archives. (We taxpayers should be gratified to know that the other ninety-seven to ninety-eight percent will be recycled into more paper.) This New England Regional Archives also does a brisk public service, helping genealogists to locate old census records and ordinary citizens to satisfy a variety of inquiries.

It was in its low-profile years—quite literally, the warehouse sits down in a hollow, below a by-way in the suburb of Waltham—that the archival collection took shape. To the core holdings—some eleven million documents belonging to JFK—were added the collected papers of other administration members and Kennedy associates, including those of RFK, also the transcripts of some 1,100 oral interviews.

Archivists wince when asked for the precise number of pages in their collections. The documents in their care are a protean mass, constantly growing at one end, being winnowed at the other and processed in between. As he prepared to make the move from Waltham to Columbia Point in 1979, Chief Archivist William Moss calculated that his material, most of it neatly filed in grey fiber Hollinger Boxes (each 4.4 inches wide) would fill most of the eighteen thousand feet of steel stacks on the seventh and eighth floors of the Library. Add to this the roughly 2.5 million pages of condolence letters—the graphic reaction to Kennedy's assassination—which remain in a nearby warehouse, and the total is thirty million pages of documents. These range in importance from four hundred boxes of National Security Files to four thousand doodles.

The enormity of the archival source material is a sign of our times. Research archivist Will Johnson points out that "the papers of the twenty-three presidents in the Library of Congress add up to two million documents. The papers of FDR alone amount to five million. Kennedy's were fifteen million and Lyndon Johnson's totaled twenty million.

HOW ARCHIVES DIFFER FROM LIBRARIES

"There is no accurate description of this place because it isn't quite like any other place," observes Bill Moss, pointing out that the word "library" implies a place to borrow, or at least to read books. To be sure there are books here—fifteen thousand volumes, plus thousands more magazine articles. But then there are the raw records of the Kennedy years, and records are, by nature, more difficult to work with than books. Library director Dan Fenn compares this kind of research to a mining operation in which researchers sift through rich lodes, gaining understanding and occasionally a few nuggets not published anywhere else. Of course you have to be able to recognize this treasure when you find it, let alone know where and how to dig.

If you wish to research a specific event—the Cuban Missile Crisis for instance—you will find the subject neatly catalogued in the third floor research room, but only in so far as it is treated in the oral histories and "printed materials." Much more on the subject is undoubtedly to be found in the president's office files and the national security files, not to mention the White House staff files and the collections of personal papers. A variety of finding aids cover each of these collections but the quality of what the researcher finds is determined largely by his tenacity and skill.

"We want to reach out farther than archives generally do," says Bill Moss. "We want to make the highschool student as welcome as the senior scholar, provided we can make it mutually beneficial... there is a nice line to walk between overselling and being too reticent about what we have to offer..."

The point is that many of the 104,276 students enrolled in the forty-six colleges and universities within public transport of Columbia Point are potential researchers.

Despite its low profile and inaccessibility by public transport, the research room in Waltham logged sixteen hundred researchers between 1969 and 1979, roughly half of them drawn from a distance. Gerard Rice from Glasgow, Scotland spent more than a year here studying the Peace Corps.

He explains: "In 1978 I was awarded a Kennedy Scholarship by the British Kennedy Memorial Trust. This body, chaired by Lord Harlech, was established with contributions from the British public. Every year the Trust sends ten British students to Harvard or MIT for one year's study in politics, philosphy or economics... these studies are not directly related to the Kennedy administration (that was sheer coincidence in my case). Rice spent his year at Harvard, much of it at the Library reading oral histories: "in many ways... my most valuable source," providing "a depth and a sparkle to my study." He writes:

> The Kennedy Papers themselves proved useful in many respects. For instance, I found some highly illuminating correspondence between Sargent Shriver and the President in the President's Office Files. Again, the personal papers of William Josephson (the Peace Corps' general counsel) provided as comprehensive a record of the Peace Corps' activities as one could hope to find... The Central Subject Files provided me with less useful information..BUT even here..in (its) bowels..I found a very interesting

Visitors to the JFK/RFK exhibit area can look up from the great pavilion and see the Kennedy Library's least visible but perhaps most important aspect: the floors where the archives are stored and scholars and researchers work.

The Kennedy Library contains far more documents, photos, records, and artifacts than books—one of the things distinguishing it from an ordinary library. But, its resources also include almost every book written on the Kennedy Family and President Kennedy's "New Frontier" era.

(Photo: S. Carothers)

memorandum from Stanley Grogan, Deputy-Director of CIA, to Pierre Salinger explaining that the CIA had nothing to do with the Peace Corps. CIA involvement was one of the most common charges against the Peace Corps by its critics. Thus, for my purposes, this memo was a real "find."

During our own research at the Library, we frequently found ourselves sitting next to LBJ biographer Doris Kearns, who had spent two and a half years worth of mornings here, researching her upcoming book about three generations of the Kennedy family, beginning with Honey Fitz and his era, ending with John Fitzgerald. Doris Kearns, who had taught a course on the Presidency at Harvard for nine years, began by reading oral histories of dozens of Boston politicians then went on to interview them herself. She read campaign files, correspondence, books by Kennedys about Kennedys, and then sought out the people who appear in these sources.

More than seventy books, magazine articles and doctoral dissertations had been researched at the Library before its move to incomparably more sumptuous and accessible quarters at Columbia Point in April, 1980. Here the names on the daily sign-in sheet are quickly multiplying, continuing to include both student researchers and eminent authors.

THE PAPERS OF PRESIDENT KENNEDY

This is the core of the archival holdings—some eleven million pages of papers ranging from early school report cards and letters home to national security files. The documents have been divided into four sub-collections.

PERSONAL PAPERS

In this forty thousand page collection you discover that John Kennedy's report card from Riverdale Country Day School showed an average of C+, that at Canterbury (a Catholic prep school) his paper on Francis I earned a D+ and that he graduated from Choate sixty-fifth in a class of one hundred and ten. Among his Harvard records you find a warning from his Winthrop House tutor about "entertaining lady guests without permission" and a wealth of notes from courses in history and government, also a handwritten report by political science Professor Carl J. Friedrich on his thesis, "Appeasement at Munich: The Inevitable Result of the Slowness of the British Democracy to Change from a Disarmament Policy." Friedrich writes: "Fundamental premises never analyzed. Much too long, wordy... thesis shows real interest and reasonable amount of work, though labor of condensation would have helped, many typographical errors." The paper had been rated magna cum laude by Kennedy's thesis advisor but Friedrich scratched that out and wrote "cum laude plus." (The thesis became Why England Slept, a book of the month club selection which sold eighty thousand copies and made forty thousand dollars in royalties.) Here you also find the diary of a trip to Europe with Choate and Princeton (Kennedy had attended for one term) friend Lem Billings. That was the summer of 1937 after Kennedy's freshman year at Harvard and after Lem's father had died, leaving him pressed for spare cash. The two boys did the grand tour on the cheap, hiding their car around the corner when they went into pensions to negotiate their nightly rate (usually forty cents).

Here, too, are the manuscripts of JFK's books: Why England Slept, As We Remember Joe (privately printed in 1945), Profiles in Courage (1956, reissued in 1960) and A Nation of Imigrants (appeared first in 1958 as a forty page pamphlet published by the Anti-Defamation League of B'nai B'rith). The collection also includes Kennedy's Senators' notes, his correspondence from 1940–1952 and four thousand doodles preserved by his secretary Evelyn Lincoln.

PRE-PRESIDENTIAL PAPERS

There are some eight hundred and sixty thousand pages of records from John Kennedy's days as a congressman and senator. These include disappointingly few papers from the 1946 campaign but plenty from the 1952 run for the United States Senate, the 1958 campaign for the same seat (for political control of the state) and the 1960 assault on the presidency. Kennedy's "transition files," including post-election correspondence and task force reports are here too. You can read a memo from Clark Clifford on a conference between President Eisenhower and the then president-elect, warning that "Laos is the present key to the entire area of Southeast Asia," also revealing that "At the present time, we are helping train anti-Castro forces in Guatemala. It was his (Eisenhower's) recommendation that this effort be continued and accelerated."

The Kennedy Library research room. Here students and scholars can study documents from the presidential archives and other collections of Kennedy papers as well as browse among the books dealing with the Kennedys and their times which are kept on open shelves.

PRESIDENTIAL PAPERS

Of course it is the Presidential Papers—some seven million pages—which chiefly interest researchers. Kennedy attempted to involve himself personally in almost every major issue and was daily bombarded with memos and letters on an extraordinary range of subjects.

These papers logically divide into eight distinct collections, beginning with the President's Office Files—the working files kept by the president's secretary Evelyn Lincoln. The series titled "special correspondence" contains letters such as the one from John Kenneth Galbraith as Ambassador to India (November 23, 1961) already describing Vietnam as "a can of snakes"; John Steinbeck's letter, forwarded by Adlai Stevenson, requesting that the novelist be appointed "Ambassador to Oz," and the note from former president Harry Truman (August of 1962) advising Kennedy: "don't let these damned columnists and editorial writers discourage you... You meet 'em, cuss 'em and give 'em hell and you'll win in 1964."

And there is the letter from Robert Frost (July, 1962) thanking "my dear Mr. President" for taking "the chance of sending anyone like me over there affinitizing with the Russians... I am almost as full of politics and history as you are... I shall be reading poems chiefly over there but I shall be talking some where I read and you may be sure I won't be talking just literature." This fascinating collection—filed by the name of the correspondent and also by people discussed—includes letters from Herbert Hoover, Dwight Eisenhower, Pope John XXIII, Eleanor Roosevelt and Pablo Casals.

Research archivist Will Johnson notes that "although nominally the papers of an individual," the presidential papers "are every bit as staggering in their size and diversity as the records of any major organization." In addition to Special Correspondence, his Office Files alone include "General Correspondence" (Kennedy received thousands of letters a day), his "Speech Files" (incomplete but containing rough drafts of many of JFK's most famous addresses), "Legislative Files" (an incomplete series of reports and memoranda documenting the attempt to get programs through Congress), his "Press Conferences" (some of them), "Staff Memoranda" and "Departments and Agencies."

Then there are the National Security Files, four hundred boxes of working files belonging to McGeorge Bundy, special assistant to the President for National Security Affairs. Obviously this collection contains most of the Archives's classified material.

At present some seven hundred and fifty thousand documents remain closed for national security reasons but a researcher can request "mandatory review" of a classified document described in library finding aids. Thanks to an executive order enacted in 1978 the number of classified documents will also shrink appreciably through "systematic review": all documents must now be reviewed for declassification once they are twenty years old. The Kennedy Library actually has a grace period; all its classified material must be reviewed by 1988.

There is a wealth of material to be found in the National Security Files as they stand: besides two hundred and eleven boxes full of documents indexed by country there are twenty-two boxes on Regional Security (e.g. "Southeast Asia" and "NATO"), twenty-one boxes on "Meetings and Memoranda" (among the most popular research sources since this series contains minutes of National Security Council meetings).

Then there are the elaborate White House central subject files, a record of the presidential bureaucracy: name files of copies of incoming correspondence, chronological files of outgoing documents, subject files and classified files.

Dull as this all sounds in bulk, it is fascinating when you go searching for something in particular. You can pick any incident depicted in the museum (the exhibit area is, after all, a showcase for the archives) and pursue it.

Among the exhibits you will find, for instance, a memo indicating that President Kennedy wondered out loud why there were no black faces in the Coast Guard's honor guard at his inauguration; the memo (January 25, 1961) to presidential aid Richard Goodwin reveals that: "There are currently no Negro cadets in the United States Coast Guard Academy." Salted away in the White House Central Files it is possible to find a total of seven more documents which follow this story through to its end: the appointment of the first Negro to the Coast Guard Academy in 1962.

Finally there are the condolence letters, two million, six hundred thousand letters, many from such unexpected places as the Ilford Jewish Youth Club in Ilford, Essex (England). There are some four thousand formal condolences from foreign governments, state assemblies and organizations, obviously deeply felt. Indira Gandhi, prime minister of India wrote:

"I wonder if there is another instance in history when a single individual symbolized the hopes and aspirations of such divergent groups... it was the warmth and essential humaneness of his personality which evoked friendship and affection."

Winston Churchill, in a personal note to Jackie Kennedy, writes:

"Never have I been so filled with revulsion, anger and sorrow as when I heard of your husband's death. On this great and good man were set the hopes of humanity... All men who prize freedom and hope for peace share your loss and partake of your grief."

There are boxes of poems written to express grief of people ranging from six year olds to Pulitzer prize-winning poets. There are some four thousand pieces of music in manuscript and printed form, some four thousand essays and magazine articles on the president's death and some two thousand sermons inspired by it.

While the bulk of the condolence letters are stored in a Hingham warehouse, twenty boxes are kept at the Library. These include a letter to Mrs. Kennedy and the children from a sixteen year old Cerebral Palsy victim in Denver. He wrote: "I felt like I could almost stand alone when he talked to us Americans..." A fourteen year old girl wrote about how Kennedy made her realize that she could do more to help other people: "I mean if you take a look at yourself and really think for the first time that maybe you could help someone if you really wanted to."

WHAT'S INVOLVED IN PROCESSING

The myriad papers—the raw material from which future pictures of the Kennedy years will be pieced—arrived at the Library's Waltham quarters in a variety of shapes. The White House Central Files came in 1969, already neatly indexed and filed. Ernest Hemingway's eight hundred and fifty-eight manuscripts, ten thousand photos and some eleven hundred letters plus scrapbooks arrived in dribs and drabs, in wooden crates, boxes, file cabinets and shopping bags. Robert Kennedy's records, packed in a thousand boxes (documents are initially packed in cubic foot boxes, each holding roughly two thousand pages) began arriving in 1969 and "personal collections" are still being acquired. Acquisitions officer Robert Stocking's job entails periodic forages through the cellars and attics of former New Frontiersmen. Collections thus unearthed in old trunks and supermarket cartons have ranged from one to three thousand boxes (again the cubic foot variety).

"Think of these boxes as the ropes with which anthropologists mark off a "dig" advises RFK curator Henry Gwiazda. Next papers are placed in the smaller Hollinger boxes but remain grouped by origin (among Robert Kennedy's papers are some of Joseph P. Kennedy's records from his service on the Hoover Commission. They remain with the Robert Kennedy papers because that is where the archivists found them, and the assumption is that Robert Kennedy felt that they were his, or was at least using them for some purpose).

Papers are read carefully. A small percentage which were already classified when they arrived, are stowed in the vault for safekeeping. Most are Xeroxed (the original papers would disintegrate with time), staples are removed (steel ions eventually create acid, destroying the papers they hold) and papers are restapled with brass; folders are discarded for acid-free folders. Next the materials must be listed in "registers" (a folder title list). Folders are grouped into homogeneous "series" which are titled descriptively. The register also includes an introduction about the origin of the collection and the person or organization that produced the papers. These registers are usually contained in large loose-leaf binders which sit on open shelves in the third floor research room.

COLLECTIONS OF PERSONAL OR ORGANIZATIONAL DOCUMENTS

This portion of the archives will be more illuminating in another fifty years or so. Most of the public figures whose papers have already been deposited in the Library are still too active to permit opening their records to public perusal. And there will be many more such collections to come. Of the more than one hundred and fifty now held by the library, more than one third are still closed and another dozen require special permission to look at.

The variety of people represented here is fascinating. Most are statesmen recruited by John Kennedy—Secretary of Agriculture Orville Freeman, Presidential Advisor Clark Clifford and Secretary of the Treasury Douglas Dillon; there are also some of Kennedy's old school friends like Lemoyne

The attractive JFK Library research room is closed to the general public but can be used by anyone doing research, from a high school student writing a paper to an eminent political scientist working on a book.

(Photo: S. Carothers)

Billings and Torbert MacDonald. There are authors who have written about Kennedys (Arthur Schlesinger and Theodore Sorensen among others), authors who wrote for them (speechwriter Richard Goodwin), authors who involved them in research about other people (Frank Cormier who wrote Reuther and Walter Sheridan who wrote The Fall and Rise of Jimmy Hoffa.

The papers of New Frontiersmen most frequently used by researchers are those of John Kenneth Galbraith—a tremendous trove of material ranging from trenchant memos to book manuscripts—and those of Burke Marshall, assistant attorney general for civil rights.

The records of a few organizations are also here, notably more than two million pages of documents belonging to the Democratic National Committee. Small collections belong to the Bedford-Stuyvesant Corporation (RFK's concern) and the Vietnamese American Association (sixty-four rolls of microfilm about the Nguyen Dynasty from 1802–1860).

There are also personal collections which seem to have nothing to do with John F. Kennedy at all—those of Louis Brownlow (a journalist and public administrator during the Roosevelt Administration) and James Warburg, an economic advisor to Franklin Roosevelt.

And there are the papers of Ernest Hemingway, here by special arrangement between Hemingway's widow Mary and Jacqueline Kennedy. The size and nature of this collection, along with that of Robert Kennedy, merit their own curator in the library and a special treatment in this book.

This handwritten memo from economic adviser Walter Heller to JFK is typical of the kind of once highly confidential material which is accessible to researchers at the Kennedy Library.

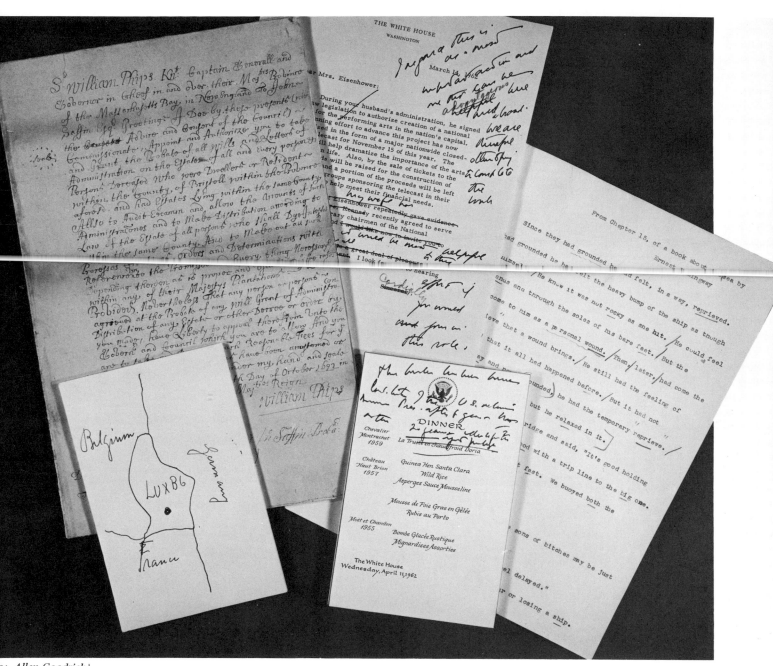

The Kennedy Library archives contain an extraordinary range of documents, from notes and doodles to historic documents and state papers. Shown are, from left, a doodle JFK dashed off during a state dinner for the Grand Duchess of Luxembourg; a 17th Century document from Kennedy's personal collection; a draft of a letter to Mrs. Dwight Eisenhower with handwritten corrections; a White House dinner menu; and a page of an unpublished Hemingway manuscript.

FROM THE DESK OF
HARRY S. TRUMAN   8-11-62

Privat & confidential.

Mr. President don't let these damned columnists and editorial writers discourage you.

In my opinion you are on the right track.

The President is just as great as the Congress — and really greater — when he exercices his Const.tutional Prerogatives.

You are going through the same situations and troubles that Franklin Roosevelt, Abraham Lincoln and I had to meet. Don't like to put myself in that high class — but I had a hell of a time.

"Mr. President don't let those damned columnists and editorial writers discourage you..." Harry Truman, who certainly had his share of press criticism, urged JFK to hold fast to his constitutional prerogatives: "...in my opinion you are on the right track." Originally "private and confidential" the memo can now be studied by researchers.

President Kennedy carefully edited and often rewrote important speeches, such as this famous address delivered in West Berlin in 1963 when he declared: "I am a Berliner..."

6/25/63 3rd draft rev

Mr. Chancellor, Mr. Mayor, Citizens of Berlin:

Fifteen years ago this very day an airplane traveling from Wiesbaden to Berlin, the route I followed this morning, started the airlift -- to supply a free city against a cruel blockade. Many believed that the blockade would end this city's life -- but the city survived and prospered.

Ten years ago this month a spontaneous uprising of the freedom-loving people in the Eastern Zone was repressed. Many believed that this tragic result would crush all hope for freedom among the East Germans -- but those hopes are vigorously alive today.

Almost five years ago the people of West Berlin were warned that their present status would end, and two years ago a shameful wall was built. Many believed that this warning and this wall would drain the life from West Berlin. But today there are more people in West Berlin -- with more vitality, and more courage -- than ever before.

The story of West Berlin is many stories -- valor, danger, honor, determination, unity and hardship. But, above all, it is the story of achievement.

From a ruin of rubble you have made a glowing center of free life.

I will carry away from this City an inspiring picture of all I have seen.

90

Writing from Harvard University, where he was professor of economics, John Kenneth Galbraith offered JFK strategic and policy advice on political and economic matters, such as the danger of predicting a business up-turn that might not happen.

JOHN KENNETH GALBRAITH
HARVARD UNIVERSITY
CAMBRIDGE, MASSACHUSETTS

February 13, 1961

President John F. Kennedy
The White House
Washington, D. C.

Dear Mr. President:

Here are some weekend thoughts:

(1) I haven't been much enchanted by this trip of Arthur Goldberg's. Obviously one doesn't learn anything by visiting unemployed families in Detroit that isn't known or cannot otherwise be learned. So it is a gimmick and a slightly transparent one that makes capital out of misfortune. I suggest that after all of these years of Eisenhower, the rule should be: Nothing Contrived, Nothing Bogus. And nothing is so important as your reputation for playing it straight.

(2) I think it might be worthwhile quietly to caution top members of the Administration against predicting a business upturn. (I have seen two or three optimistic statements in recent days.) No one really knows. If anything is certain, it is that one cannot talk business into a recovery. And nothing brings more discredit than promises of recovery à la Hoover that ....

(3) I sense that you are tapering off on the live television. This I would strongly endorse. If the taped performances could be spaced out, this too would be fine. My notion is that television exposure must be rationed for maximum effect. The time will doubtless come when you will need such effect.

(4) Economic and business comment on the economic and balance-of-payments messages has, I think, been favorable. Their moderation is taken as reassuring proof that my influence has been slight.

(5) Is someone riding herd on the Departments to make sure that all the promised legislation is getting up to the Hill promptly?

Yours faithfully,

J. K. Galbraith

JKG/adw

New Delhi, India,

November 28, 1961.

ITS-9

Dear Mr. President:

You will already have had sundry more official communications from me on South Viet Nam. This is by way of giving you something of the informal flavor and color of the local scene.

It is certainly a can of snakes. I am reasonably accustomed to oriental government and politics, but I was not quite prepared for Diem. As you will doubtless be warned, whenever anyone reaches an inconvenient conclusion on this country, he has been duped. My view is derived neither from the Indians nor the Saigon intellectuals but my personal capacity for error. One of the proposals which I am told was made to Max Taylor provides an interesting clue to our man. It was that a helicopter be provided to pluck him out of his palace and take him directly to the airport. This is because his surface travel through Saigon requires the taking in of all laundry along the route, the closing of all windows, an order to the populace to keep their heads in, the clearing of all streets, and a vast bevy of motorcycle outriders to protect him on his dash. Every trip to the airport requires such arrangements and it is felt that a chopper would make him seem more democratic. Incidentally, if Diem leaves town for a day,

The President,

The White House.

Noted economist and key New Frontiersman John Kenneth Galbraith advised President Kennedy on a variety of issues. In this 1961 memo, written when he was United States ambassador to India, he criticized President Diem and his government and labeled the situation in South Viet Nam: "... a can of snakes."

ERNEST HEMINGWAY

John F. Kennedy and Ernest Hemingway admired each other immensely. Both were men in a hurry to live life to its fullest, as they perceived it. They shared a fascination with courage. Both had proven their own mettle under fire, Hemingway in repeated war-time sallies, beginning with ambulance service in World War I at the age of eighteen. Both men went on to write about courage, both winning Pulitzer Prizes in the process. One man was famed ultimately for his "grace under pressure" and the other for his novels about this virtue.

Hemingway's words have often been used to describe Kennedy. A Thousand Days, Arthur Schlesinger's biography about Kennedy and his administration, is prefaced by a quotation from Hemingway's Farewell to Arms:

> If people bring so much courage
> to this world the world has to kill
> them to break them, so of course
> it kills them. The world breaks
> everyone and afterward many are
> strong at the broken places. But
> those that will not break, it kills.
> It kills the very good and the
> very gentle and the very brave
> impartially.

Unfortunately, by the time Kennedy assumed office Hemingway was ill; he died, aged sixty-two, in July of 1961. As a tribute the president had Fredric March read a long passage from Islands in The Sea (unpublished at the time) at his dinner for Nobel Prize winners.

"Papa" in his prime. This photograph was taken in Sun Valley in 1939 when Hemingway was finishing "For Whom the Bell Tolls."

In the Library itself there is no permanent Hemingway exhibit. But researchers are invited to use the fourth floor Hemingway Room, its shelves filled with reference material and mementoes such as Hemingway's hunting trophies and high school diploma.

It was in 1972 that the Hemingway papers themselves began arriving at the Library's Waltham quarters. They came in a more chaotic state than anything yet received from politicians. They came in shopping bags and in wooden crates. They came from Idaho and New York, from Havana and Key West (some of these from the back room at Sloppy Joe's Bar).

In all there are now eight hundred and fifty-eight manuscripts (forty thousand pages) of works ranging from poems to thick novels. There are also eleven hundred letters, most of them to Hemingway's fellow literati such as Thornton Wilder, William Carlos Williams, John Dos Passos, Ezra Pound, Gertrude Stein, William Faulkner, H. L. Mencken, Bernard De Voto and Scott Fitzgerald.

"Hemingway was a packrat," observes curator of his papers Jo August. "He kept everything: hotel receipts, passports, a fishing license from his 1923 trip to Spain..."

There are scrapbooks documenting Hemingway's boyhood, books belonging to him, translations of his own books and works generated by research on this collection—which constitutes ninety percent of the author's papers and is substantially open to researchers.

The audio-visual collection here is an important complement to the papers. There are more than ten thousand photographs, many of them wartime pictures taken by Hemingway himself. Many of them are utilized in the moving NBC documentary on the author narrated by Chet Huntley.

This tells the story of a boy born in 1899 into a large, well-to-do family near Chicago, one who plunged from public high school into the rough and tumble assignments of a general reporter for the Kansas (Missouri) Star, then hastened into World War I (due to a weakness in one eye, the result of a high school boxing accident, he had to settle for duty with the American Field Service). He soon suffered a leg wound while trying to evacuate a wounded soldier. He was already an extremely verile-looking hero living the stuff of which novels are made.

During the next six years, years mostly spent in Europe as a badly paid correspondent for the Toronto Star, Hemingway mingled in Paris with other writers of "the lost generation" and gradually struck his own stride as an author. It was in 1926 that The Sun Also Rises was published and became an instant success. He was just twenty-six years old. For the next three decades he was to be one of the most widely read, certainly the most widely watched, of the century's writers.

His life itself continued to resemble fiction. Divorcing his first wife in 1927, he married a Vogue fashion editor in Paris, then moved to Key West (where his home is now open to the public) and wrote Farewell to Arms, Death in the Afternoon and The Green Hills of Africa, among other things. In 1937

he plunged into the Spanish Civil War as a correspondent for the North American Newspaper Alliance. For Whom the Bell Tolls expresses this deeply felt experience.

In 1939 Hemingway moved to Havana (his home base until 1960) and the next year he was divorced again, married to another newspaper correspondent, one with whom he competed in the coverage of the Sino-Japanese War and of the final phase of World War II. He continued to be prolific and almost every book was an instant success; most of them were made into movies. By 1946 when he married journalist Mary Welsh, his final wife, he had already acquired a grandfatherly image and the nickname "Papa." He continued to write novels and short stories into the mid-fifties, receiving his Pulitzer for The Old Man and The Sea, set in Cuba.

Since Hemingway shared with JFK an intense love of the sea, it is extremely fitting that his memory should be preserved primarily here by Dorchester Bay. The Library's first major Hemingway conference was actually held on one of the Boston Harbor Islands.

A table a trois. Hemingway sits between his first wife Hadley and Pauline Pfeiffer, who was to be his second wife, at a cafe in Pamplona in 1926. At left, are Gerald and Sara Murphy, a well-to-do American couple whose Paris studio Hemingway often frequented.

As a war correspondent in the last days of World War II, Hemingway gets a briefing from Colonel "Buck" Lanham. In the foreground is the wreckage of a German 88.

(Photo: John Fitzgerald Kennedy Library)

Another Pamplona cafe scene. Hemingway is at left, first wife Hadley in the middle.

Now an authentic "Old Man of the Sea" himself, Hemingway acted as a technical advisor when his prize-winning novel—set in Cuba—was filmed off the coast of Peru.

Looking like a latter day Huck Finn, the young Ernest Hemingway posed with his kill in the Upper Peninsula of Michigan. Photo was taken on the shore of Walloon Lake in 1913.

Hemingway wrote about fishing with the authority of experience. Here he poses with a marlin, one of many he caught off Cuba and Florida.

Robert on the lawn of the Kennedy family home in Hyannisport, Massachusetts, in the 1930's.

ROBERT F. KENNEDY

While President Kennedy himself had no hand in the actual shaping of his library, Robert Kennedy did.

Of all the family and friends involved in the library's inception, Robert was the most active. He was the first president of the Kennedy Library Corporation. He signed all letters sent out requesting interviews for the oral history project and donations of papers to the Library. He headed up the ten million dollar fund drive, an effort as complicated as any campaign, with committees in every state. To ensure full support and input from fellow New Frontiersmen, he wrote hundreds of letters such as this one to former Secretary of State Dean Rusk:

> I know this project will be a drain on your time and resources. But only in this way can we hope to build a collection which accurately reflects the career, the hopes, and the achievements of President Kennedy and which fully illuminates the issues of his time. I know you share my desire that the Library be worthy of his own standards of accuracy, completeness, and intellectual integrity.

For TV personality Jack Paar (sic) in February, 1964, he defined the thrust of the Library as he hoped it would be:

> There's going to be a good deal of emphasis on political life... that it's not a bad profession... and that in order to make... government in the country better... people have to take an interest in politics and participate...

The following month a newspaper columnist noted, "Robert Kennedy is calling all the shots in the Kennedy Library." By June of 1968, when he was assassinated, the necessary funding had been secured and the nature of the library had been determined.

It is fitting that material about Robert Kennedy forms the second largest collection within the Library. In addition to his papers, it includes a distinct oral history project focusing on his life and career (one hundred and fifty interviews to date), nine thousand, five hundred and sixty photographs, five hundred and sixty thousand feet of motion picture film, two hundred and thirty-five sound recordings and twelve hundred three-dimensional objects.

The RFK papers alone total two million pages. Since these came to the Library five years after the President's papers, work on the Attorney General's papers is still continuing. According to RFK curator Dr. Henry Gwiazda, there are still eight hundred more cubic foot cartons from the Senate and 1968 campaign to open.

What researchers can peruse now are Robert Kennedy's papers from his years as a Senate investigation counsel and a political campaign manager in 1960, also his correspondence as Attorney General. Kennedy's role as counsel for the Senate's "McCarthy and McClellan" committees is widely misunderstood and researching it makes fresh, fascinating reading.

Robert Kennedy's job in 1952 was assistant counsel to Joe McCarthy on the Permanent Sub-committee on Investigations of the Senate Government Operations Committee. While the committee is notorious for its "witch hunts" for communists, RFK was involved only in investigating the amount of shipping trade being carried on between American allies and Communist China during the Korean War. He was able to prove that seventy-five percent of all ships carrying freight to China at this time were flying the flags of our professed allies. After submitting his report, Kennedy resigned from the committee. At this juncture he received a letter from Senator Stuart Symington:

> Your investigation into the details of shipping... along with your subsequent testimony before the Committee and your work on the final report, in my opinion, is one of the two outstanding jobs I have seen done in committee work during

MARCH 13, 1968

Dear Tony,

I appreciated hearing from you as both Ethel and I always do.

I don't know quite what to write to you. The country is in such difficulty and I believe headed for even more that it almost fills one with despair. I just don't know what Johnson is thinking. But then when I realize all of that I wonder what I should be doing. Most everyone who I respect with the exception of Dick Goodwin & Arthur Schlesinger

Letter written to Anthony Lewis of the New York Times in March of 1968 in which RFK expresses concern and near despair about the state of the country, and suggests he is considering a presidential bid.

One explanation or answer that Hoffa invariably gives

to the corruption within his union is that "I get good contracts

for my men." With this answer he endeavors to excuse everything

wrong within the Teamsters Union. Even if it were true it could

be no explanation. The fact is though, that it is not true.

The Committee went extensively into the contracts nego-

tiated by Hoffa and the Central Conference of Teamsters and compared

them with contracts in the eastern section of the U. S. We

found the contracts negotiated by Hoffa were not as good for the

employees as far as wages, hours and conditions, as were the con-

tracts that were negotiated by union officials over whom he has

had no control.

Furthermore, we found that many of the contracts for

the largest carriers in the Central Conference of Teamsters

are not being enforced. We found that Mr. Hoffa, in his attempts

to gain power and increase his area of control, offered

[handwritten left margin:] many of the contracts negotiated by Hoffa in Hoffa's home city are substandard contracts or are below sub standard. In Ohio over which he had no control up until the early 1950 he has been trying to retard the rate of increase negotiated by honest union officials so that his own contracts will be less out of line.

[handwritten edits:] other sections / one are not / in other sections of the country / Same para

[handwritten bottom:] has gone into areas outside his jurisdiction & offered attractive deals to employers to tie them up & thus undermine & destroy the local union officials there

-1-

some eight years I have been in Washington.

When Robert Kennedy returned to this sub-committee the following year it was as minority counsel for Democratic Senators Henry Jackson, Stuart Symington and John McClellan. He was soon involved in the Army/McCarthy Hearings and drafted a main part of the report critical of McCarthy. This particular inquiry was televised; the senate censured McCarthy and his public image was destroyed. Robert Kennedy subsequently became chief counsel for the Committee, refocusing its efforts on waste and graft in the government, exposing, for example, Harold Talbott—Eisenhower's Secretary of the Air Force—for directing military business to his own firm.

After a brief time out for campaigning with Adlai Stevenson in 1956, RFK spent three years investigating labor racketeers. Since his elder brother was a member of the "Select Committee on Improper Activities in the Labor Management Field," for which RFK now served as counsel, the two brothers were frequently confused by the public. RFK was primarily responsible for the investigation and resignation of teamster boss Dave Beck and for repeated attempts to convict Jimmy Hoffa.

By 1959, Robert Kennedy was discouraged about the growing strength of organized crime. In a memorandum he noted that: "in the months since the committee began work, conditions in the labor and management fields have actually grown worse." To convey the threatening power of organized crime in America, he wrote (with the help of journalist John Seigenthaler) a best seller, The Enemy Within.

Robert Kennedy's role in his brother's campaigns—congressional, senatorial and presidential—is well known. His position within his brother's administration is, however, less widely appreciated.

In an oral history interview with Anthony Lewis (Dec. 4, 1964) RFK said: "I did not so much want to become attorney general as to be around during that time."

Robert turned thirty-five years old two months before moving into his paneled new office, which he characteristically plastered with drawings by his children. As attorney general he was to win praise for his handling of civil rights crises, for his programs to combat juvenile delinquency and organized crime and for efforts to have the poor receive equal treatment in the courts. He also became deeply involved in foreign policy decisions, circling the globe on fact-finding missions and writing a book to express his views (Just Friends and Brave Enemies).

The papers from RFK's years as New York senator await processing. Oral histories, however, help fill in this period. There is a tribute, for instance, from migrant worker leader Cesar Chavez, recalling the senator's visit to Delano, California early in 1966.

> He said we had the right to form a union and that he endorsed our right, and not only endorsed us but joined us. I was amazed at how quickly he grasped the whole picture...He immediately asked very pointed questions of the growers; he had a way of disintegrating their arguments by picking at the very simple questions...When reporters asked him if we weren't Communists, he said: "No, they are not Communists, they're struggling for their rights." So he really helped us...turned it completely around...

Robert Kennedy was forty-two years old in 1968, the father of eleven children and a host of programs to fight poverty and injustice. His own words, the final ones of his postscript in To Seek A Newer World, his last book, best express what his life itself conveyed:

> Our future may lie beyond our vision, but it is not completely beyond our control. It is the shaping impulse of America that neither fate nor nature nor the irresistible tides of history, but the work of our own hands, matched to reason and principle, that will

determine destiny. There is pride in that, even arrogance, but there is also experience and truth. In any event, it is the only way we can live.

AUDIO VISUAL COLLECTION

The Library's audio visual collection began with the eight fat file cabinets full of photos by White House photographers which were transferred abruptly to the National Archives when LBJ took office. Roughly seventy percent of these pictures are of the president himself and the remainder, his family.

Add to these the photos of President Kennedy donated to the Library by various government agencies, by newspapers, magazines and wire services. Also add the nine thousand, five hundred and sixty photos of RFK, ten thousand of Ernest Hemingway and a scattering of small photo collections belonging to other notables and the Library's still photographs now total more than one hundred and fifteen thousand. A large percentage of these prints are in the public domain and another large percentage are negotiable, constituting a genuine resource on which writers and publishers draw heavily.

For the researcher, however, the film and sound tape collections are more intriguing.

"What we have here in the making," says Allan Goodrich, curator of the audio-visual collection, "is the country's best source of political film—almost from its inception—from the beginning of network news coverage of campaigns, up into the mid-sixties."

There are some six million, five hundred thousand feet of motion picture film, two million, five hundred thousand feet of it donated by the major TV networks and others (some of it dating back to JFK's congressional days, but most of it depicting the president's trips and speeches). There is another two million, five hundred thousand feet of film produced by Guggenheim Productions, the highly respected political film firm responsible for promoting presidential

hopefuls from Adlai Stevenson to Edward Kennedy. Besides spots produced for JFK and RFK there are similar commercials for dozens of other politicians. It was Guggenheim who produced "John F. Kennedy, 1917–1963" the film introducing visitors to the Library's exhibits. They also earned an Oscar for "RFK Remembered," the documentary prepared in just two months time for the 1968 Democratic Convention (a clip from this is shown within the RFK museum exhibits).

There is also the Victoria Schuck collection, primarily TV and audio spots produced by both parties between 1950 and 1968 (Ms. Schuck, president of Mt. Vernon College in Washington, DC, assembled this material while a professor of political science at Mount Holyoke College). The Democratic National Committee has also deposited film covering its 1953–1963 campaigns and conventions.

Much of this film is, however, subject to copyright restrictions and most of it is unavailable to researchers until preservation copies can be made of the original films. Priority in this processing has been given to JFK's speeches and press conferences.

"We are the victims of inflation," observes Curator Goodrich, explaining that back in 1970–1971, Congress voted one million dollars annually for processing audio-visual collections at all the presidential libraries. It would take one million dollars just to reproduce the present film holdings in this library, he says.

What is readily available—either to view in the Library's second floor research room or to show to groups on a rental basis—are small feature films such as "A Thousand Days" (produced by Wolper Productions for the 1964 Democratic Convention), the Kennedy-Nixon Debates, JFK's press conference of November 20, 1962 and his address to the Greater Houston Ministerial Association.

There are also four thousand, five hundred sound recordings, notably two hundred and forty-four tapes of presidential addresses and remarks recorded by the White House Communications Agency (WHCA) between

FINAL

Long Island Sunday Press

10¢

137th YEAR — No. 47 — SUNDAY, FEBRUARY 17, 1957 — Entered as Second Class Matter At Flushing, Jamaica, N.Y. — 126 PAGES

Union Chiefs Warned: Don't Talk To Racket Probers or You'll Die

Several Long Island union leaders testify ... rackets warned ... Death ... made over ... eral bus ... financial ... Nassau ... involved ... Though ...

turns its full spotlight on Friday ...

INVESTIGATIVE TEAM—Senator McClellan and Counsel Kennedy check documents on racketeering inquiry.

McClellan-Kennedy Team Is Set For Season's Biggest Investigation

By JAMES Y. NEWTON and CECIL HOLLAND

The big Congressional investigation of the season will get under way this week under the direction of an effective though oddly ...

on seeking out wrongdoing on the part of Government officials and agencies and those doing business with the Government.

In so doing, Senator McClellan and Mr. Kennedy have restored to ...

committee—and got $350,000 for the undertaking.

This set the stage for an inquiry which, judging by the letters pouring in to Senator McClellan and Mr. Kennedy at the rate of nearly 100 a day, is welcomed by the rank and file of labor as well as many of its leaders. For the team of McClellan and Kennedy it is an exciting challenge and an opportunity to demonstrate ... how ...

Union Racketeering Threat to Democracy

The Senate McClellan investigating committee has been delving into noisome details of alleged labor racketeering that extends even to betrayal of union members by unscrupulous leaders. The practices as described by witnesses are so extreme that a friend of organized labor, Senator Ives of New York, has held that racketeers have become a worse evil in the union movement than Communists.

challenge to the law-abiding element to clean up. However, previously the Kefauver Senate committee investigating organized crime has reported on the great power of the underworld from wealth amassed from illicit activities—power that has been turned in instances to demoralizing law enforcement. Local authorities in instances have been too impotent or too corrupt to cure the situation.

Thus, such investigations of that kind ...

Beck Didn't Borrow-- He Stole, Says Kennedy

By the Associated Press

Washington — An insurance official testified today Dave Beck did not list loans of $300,000-plus from the Teamsters Union when making a financial statement in ...

★ ★ ★

Beck Ouster Weighed

Washington — Union leaders met today to consider the possibility of toppling Dave Beck ...

conference for the purpose of discussing the scandal-scarred union's "problems in general."

AFL-CIO Kicks Out Beck For Misusing Union Cash

Unanimous Action Taken By Board

By MAUREEN GOTHLIN, *United Press Staff Writer.*

WASHINGTON, May 20.—Teamster president Dave Beck was ousted as an AFL-CIO vice president of the AFL-CIO executive council today on grounds of "gross misuse" of union funds.

The action came shortly after Beck, 62, refused at a closed-door AFL-CIO trial to answer charges that he had brought the labor movement into "disrepute."

AFL-CIO president George Meany announced that the 25 members of the executive council present today had unanimously voted Beck's ouster—an unprecedented action.

"There is not the faintest question in our minds he is completely guilty of violating trade union laws through his use of union money which is "a sacred trust," Mr. Meany said.

Appears Half Hour.

Mr. Meany said the question whether the Teamsters union chief was guilty of violating laws involving "theft or embezzlement" was not the concern of the executive council, of which Beck had been a member since August, 1953.

Beck had appeared before the council this morning for only a half hour. During his appearance, Beck refused to accept his previous suspension as an AFL-CIO vice president and council member of the AFL-CIO ...

Hoffa Accused Of Diverting Welfare Funds

Teamsters Seen Taking 50% Loss In $1 Million Deal

By LEE COHN *Star Staff Writer*

Senate investigators charged today that James R. Hoffa helped swing a complicated real estate deal that cost the Teamsters Union hundreds of thousands of dollars.

According to testimony before the Senate Rackets Committee, the welfare fund of Hoffa's Michigan Conference of Teamsters loaned $1 million to land developers in 1955.

Witnesses said the original agreement protected the union's interests, but the safeguards were waived by George S. Fitzgerald, a top lawyer for Hoffa and attorney for the welfare fund.

More Than Overalls in This Chowder

MANAGEMENT CONNIVANCE — SENATE COMMITTEE — LABOR PROBE — LATBURY

... warned from Miami found South ... said to right: Therese Hennessey, South Boston.

Eisenhower said it is possibly true that there will be fewer people in the armed services if you look far enough ahead.

And When the Pie Was Opened . . .

IT WAS ONLY A $60,000 "GIFT"! — MY "ADMIRERS" ONLY GAVE ME A HOUSE AND LOT! — MY TAKE WAS ONLY A PLUSH CAR! — $15,000 LOAN. — BAKERS' UNION — SENATE RACKETS COMMITTEE — LATBURY

Stole $5 a Member, Senate Probers Say

Hoods Got $10 Millions Out of Five Unions

(See Lyle Wilson's column on Page 18)

The Senate Rackets Committee reported today union officials, including an infiltration of "gangsters and hoodlums," have "stolen, embezzled or misused" more ... five unions.

It said the 15-year total amounts to "an average of $5 out of the pocket of every member of the unions covered" in a 12,000-word first installment of a formal report on its first year's operations.

Sen. Pat McNamara (D., Mich.), however, labelled the financial estimates an unsupported "statistical perversion." In a sharply-worded ...

... tion as a trade union official to use money belonging to dues-paying members for his own personal gain and profit.

Mr. Meany said Beck walked out of his trial this morning after reading a 500-word statement rejecting the charges.

"But before he read his statement he listened to me for 20 minutes," Mr. Meany said.

What I Thought.

Mr. Meany said he had summarized the charges for Beck and "I told him what I thought ...

... evidence against him; that the Civil Liberties group " doubt" would have accused the committee of being unfair it had denied him the right.

He added that he believes Beck "has committed many criminal offenses" and that he reserves the right "to express any views ... that is a 'civil liberty' I have not surrendered and do not intend to relinquish."

Kennedy Reports on Reform Bill, Warns of Work Ahead

By BILL LEE *(Enterprise-Record Managing Editor)*

Robert F. Kennedy, the engaging but hard-chinned younger brother of the Democratic Party's current front-runner in the 1960 presidential handicap, gave a mixed audience of 200 Democrats and Republicans a brief but detailed report on the current status of U.S. labor-

1961 and 1963. Complementing these are the radio tapes, donated by members of the National Association of Broadcasters, covering Kennedy's speeches and campaign ads from 1952 until 1963. And there are tapes of the entire 1956 and 1960 Democratic National Conventions, also a couple of hundred tapes and discs of personal memorials ranging from individuals reading their own poetry to performances by philharmonic orchestras.

Finally there are five hundred political cartoons, most of them benign since they were presented to the president by their creators. More interesting are the caricatures of Boston political figures and issues dating back to 1876.

PRINTED MATERIALS

Some fifteen thousand catalogued books are ranged on open shelves around the research room on the Library's third floor. Thousands of magazine and newspaper articles plus doctoral theses and government publications are also available here, adding up the world's most comprehensive collection of words published about John F. Kennedy, his administration and the era framing it.

There are the dozen books actually authored by John Kennedy; be it said that only Why England Slept and Profiles in Courage were actually written as books; the remainder are collections of speeches and public statements.

On special request, researchers can also read the privately printed books such as As We Remember Joe, the seventy-five page tribute prepared by JFK for his older brother, killed in 1944, aged twenty-nine, in the course of a secret mission for the Air Corps.

A montage of newspaper headlines about the Senate Rackets Committee investigation. The investigation caused a sensation and as counsel, RFK became nationally known.

John prefaces the book with a quote from Solomon which might well apply to himself: "Honorable age is not that which standeth in length of days, nor that is measured by number of years. Having fulfilled his course in a short time, he fulfilled long years."

The book, like JFK's oral histories, is a collection of recollections of Joe by friends and acquaintances ranging from his former roommate to his Cambridge landlady. It includes the transcript of a radio broadcast about a night flight made with Joe in 1943 and the recollection by Harold Laski, Joe's tutor at the London School of Economics that "he often sat in my study and submitted with that smile that was pure magic to relentless teasing about his determination to be President of the United States."

There are two more memorial books, The Fruitful Bough, edited by Edward Kennedy and about his father, Joseph P., and That Shining Hour, prepared by Pat Kennedy Lawford in memory of Robert Kennedy. All are remarkably professional and moving works.

Books on the research room shelves range from a dozen bibliographies to literally hundreds of biographies, from a half dozen photo books on the president to major works on seemingly every major issue and aspect of the administration (there are fifty-two volumes relating to the Space Program alone). There are also more than seventy books, magazine articles and dissertations based, at least in part, on research in these archives.

In happy contrast to the archives' primary material, the contents of these "printed materials" can be centrally indexed. They are superbly catalogued by subject and by author. Similar cross referencing applies to newspaper and magazine articles and a variety of bibliographies are available on subjects ranging from children's books about Kennedy to the issues of Vietnam and Civil Rights.

Cardinal Cushing with the Kennedys at the North American College in Rome; this was July, 1963, just after Vatican II.

John Kennedy had "a way of presenting himself" to the ladies of Boston who attended his campaign teas.

(Photo: John Fitzgerald Kennedy Library)

(Above)   President Kennedy felt that we had to be first in space if we wanted to survive as a nation.

Andrew Minihan, a Kennedy cousin and mayor of New Ross, Ireland, welcomed the president to the town of his ancestors.

107

(Photo: John Fitzgerald Kennedy Library)

Princess Grace of Monaco and her husband Prince Ranier were on genuinely friendly terms with the Kennedys.

ORAL HISTORIES

Kennedy biographer Arthur Schlesinger is credited with suggesting that all JFK intimates, colleagues and fellow heads of state, plus a variety of acquaintances be interviewed about the late president. His idea was to provide human color in future Kennedy portraits. That was in December 1963, just a month after the assassination. Other administration historians enthusiastically agreed and Robert Kennedy made these oral histories his special project. The idea of incorporating verbal input into the presidential libraries was nothing new but this was to be the most ambitious undertaking of its kind; it was also the only one colored by the emotion of recent, tragic death.

With the help of a two hundred and fifty thousand dollar Carnegie Foundation grant, the interviewing began in 1964. Political friends and foes alike (Khrushchev was the first statesman to contribute) were invited to plumb their memories for reflections and anecdotes about Kennedy the man and president.

Initially the interviewing was a scattershot affair with dozens of politicians and writers asking the questions. The results ranged from wooden eulogies to spontaneous and meaty revelations. By the mid-sixties, after a couple of hundred interviews had been completed, the National Archives began administering the project on a more systematic, deliberate basis and as the presidential papers were opened, interviewers began to have better background information on which to base their questions. To date more than eleven hundred interviews have been taped and transcribed and there are still more to come.

As originally conceived, taped interviews were to be part of the Library exhibits. By pressing a button you might have heard the late Cardinal Cushing nasally recounting his role in the Bay of Pigs ransom or Astronaut Alan Shepard recalling the late president's keen interest in his mission. Unfortunately the tapes lack broadcast quality; few make any sense, it turned out, if you tune in for just one minute.

Still the oral histories are among the most accessible and heavily used items in the Archives. They are beautifully cross indexed by subject and participants. Be it said that a few of the more than six hundred interviews now complete remain closed or subject to special permission from the interviewee. Since the verbatim taped transcripts have all been reviewed by these donors, a number have come back to the Library in edited shape. The tapes, on the other hand, remain unedited. Few researchers, however, take the time to hear the tapes in addition to reading the transcripts—a pity, since the tape is a truer version of the conversation.

Archivists stress that the oral histories are essentially the reflections of men and women whose memories are clouded by time and colored by the nature of the interview. Wherever possible they should be used only within the frame of other documents available within the Archives.

As verbal pictures they are fresh and compelling. The White House gardener and upholsterer and the Boston pols, Pope Paul VI and the astronauts as well as the obvious New Frontiersmen and foreign dignitaries all had revelations which make fascinating reading.

JACK KENNEDY THE STUDENT

Ralph Horton, former director of the office of organizational planning, Department of Defense, remembers Kennedy at Choate as "a very mediocre student with a flair for writing." With eleven others they were almost expelled after the headmaster denounced them as "rotten apples," he says. Horton also recalls Kennedy's attempts to exercise his mind, his saying: "I'll pick up an article, read it, force myself to lay it down, go through the entire article in my mind, bringing to memory as much as I can, and then analyzing it and attacking it and tearing it down."

Arthur Krock, former head of the New York Times' Washington News Bureau and an old family friend, remembers first meeting Jack Kennedy as a Harvard undergraduate. He found him "a thoughtful boy, so intelligent that he might develop into an intellectual, a professor, a writer of history."

Krock helped the young Kennedy to cobble his senior thesis into the best seller Why England Slept, (published in 1940, reissued in 1961). Freda Laski, widow of the prominent professor at the London School of Economics (he had tutored Jack's older brother Joe) recalls that when her husband was shown a copy of Why England Slept that: "He thought it was the book of an immature mind; that if it hadn't been written by the son of a very rich man, it wouldn't have found a publisher." She remembers that in 1946 Jack met her husband and said: "You were quite right about the book."

The late Cardinal Cushing of Boston, interviewed by Ted Kennedy: "The first impression the future president made on me (in 1946 when he was running for Congress) was his conviction that one's education was never finished. That accounts for his constant interest in the higher things of life. Every day seemed to be a school day for him in the sense that he was always improving his intellectual ability. He was a great listener and learned from many of his elders things that he would never find in books despite the fact that he was a prolific reader. Today when I preside at the commencement exercises of colleges and universities, I try to convince the graduates that commencement exercises are only a new beginning, and I present the late President as one who was so convinced of that fact that he never succumbed to the temptation that education ended with a scholastic degree."

In 1946 Jack Kennedy ran for congress. Recollections of him at this juncture are among the most vivid to be found anywhere.

Mary Colbert, chairlady of a Charlestown political organization, remembers: "He was sort of a shy fellow. You know what I mean. He wasn't a seasoned politician by any means when he came to us. He was more of the boyish type, sort of; he pulled himself back, but he always had that habit of his hands in his coat. That was one of his characteristics that we noticed more than anything, and his way of presenting himself to people. Jack sold himself."

Mrs. Colbert helped organize a tea for Jack; it was at the Knights of Columbus, presided over by Rose and Eunice Kennedy. Fifteen years later when she paid a visit to the president at the White House she found that he hadn't forgotten.

"He came out and he said 'Mary am I glad to see you,'" she recalls. They spent the next twenty minutes talking.

William DeMarco of Boston's North End swears that Kennedy never forgot his nickname ("Yammy"). "He picked up nicknames right away. And all he had to do was see you once and he remembered you the second time," says DeMarco who saw Kennedy for the first time when he was standing in a downpour, shaking hands on Hanover Street.

"He had just a very expensive suit on. He had no raincoat and it appeared as if the suit was shrivelling to bits. I mean it was raining that bad and he had no hat. I told him I could take him up to my club and introduce him to some of the boys."

Kennedy's speech went down well at Club 28. DeMarco recalls: "He sort of blended in with the people of the North End. And they sort of took a liking to this boy and they endeared him to their hearts and it just sort of went together like bread and butter."

The picture which emerges is that of an appealing diamond in the rough.

"Jack was very shy and almost afraid to talk...my first impression of him was that he was a very sick boy," recalls State Senator Robert L. Lee.

"When he talked to you, you knew he was talking to you and you knew he was listening to you...and he gave you the feeling that he wanted and needed your help, and he wasn't being a politician when he asked for it," remembers Paul Donelan, a commercial artist who handled the artwork for Kennedy's early campaign literature.

Campaign aid Patrick J. Mulkern observes:

"That little head of hair he had, and all that. The girls went for him. Every girl you met thought she was going to be Mrs. Kennedy...

Then, of course, him being sick at that time, crippled and everything else. I think that helped him a little bit.

The sympathy. The women, the women. You can't lick sympathy; and money with it..."

Mulkern, a seasoned young Boston pol, adds:

"Of course he brought a new gang into politics...the old school is on the way out. There's no question. But he knew he had the old school around him, too, you know.

His mother was the old school. No question about it."

Cambridge funeral director and State Senator Daniel O'Brien recounts how he tried to persuade Joseph P. Kennedy to discourage his son from the 1946 race; instead the elder Kennedy "coldly sat back in his chair and said: "Why you fellows are crazy. My son will be president in 1960."

By 1960 Jack Kennedy appears to be a somewhat different man. The late Supreme Court Chief Justice William Douglas relates that while he was "largely disappointed with Jack because he really had a second or third rate record as a senator," that he had a "growth factor." He says that he watched him undergo a "transformation in 1958 and become serious about seeking the presidency..."

William Randolph Hearst explains that "It was because of knowing him in the role of a young man, unmarried and full of beans that I guess I did not support him when he ran for the presidency. I just didn't think he had enough experience in life to qualify for the job..."

Friends seemed to have underestimated Kennedy's competitive spirit, amply demonstrated in a hundred tales about the presidential campaign. John Harris, Washington Bureau Chief for the Boston Globe, describes a 1959 trip to Alaska:

"This was November...Up in Alaska everywhere there's a question about weather, whether you can travel...There was a question of whether or not...Jack's plane could come in to Ketchikan.

Now in Ketchikan, they're very sensitive about...being the gateway to Alaska...And (Richard M.) Nixon had overflown it because of the weather. Well, this gives an incentive to Jack not to overfly it, and he had to take chances in order to do this...Now, you don't land in Ketchikan. You land about twenty miles away...on a little, mountainous island called Annette Island...You have to fly in from there on an amphib into Ketchikan."

Harris describes the sudden, fluke opening in the clouds through which their commercial liner was able to put down on the island, then the hair-raising ride into Ketchikan "whipped by winds, alternate snow and rain and every other damn thing." Kennedy's visit had been assumed canceled, due to the weather but when his arrival was announced by radio, the movie hall in which he was to speak quickly filled up. Harris recalls that "Jack was introduced as the next president of the United States. You were beginning to hear that sort of thing..."

The ride back in the tin goose was worse than the one in.

"You couldn't even see outside at all... and Jack said, 'If we ever hit one of those logs, we're gone.' Then he went up and sat up forward with the pilot, and he was working the windshield wipers by hand...And what do you think about his luck! Another great big plane had come through, a Pan Am, and was able to land. So we took off almost as though it had been scheduled.

This thing got around Alaska, and already he's the magic boy, you know, above the weather. When you're above the weather,

111

you're something up there in Alaska."

Arthur Krock recalls that in March of 1960 he suggested to Joseph P. Kennedy that Jack might take second place, the vice presidency, on the national ticket. The reply: "For the Kennedys it's the castle or the outhouse. Nothing in between..."

Jack Kennedy freely admitted the disproportionate time and effort demanded by campaigning. When it came to picking his cabinet he told Dean Acheson: "that one of his troubles now was that he had spent so much time in the last few years on knowing people who could help him become president, that he found he knew very few who could help him be president."

His attitude toward the "experts," the career men in the CIA and the State Department whose job it was to advise him, soured early on. In April, 1961, a force of fifteen hundred anti-Castro Cubans, trained in Guatemala with support from the CIA, invaded Cuba at the Golfo de Cochinos (Bay of Pigs). Way outnumbered by Castro's forces, the men were killed or imprisoned. The plan had been entirely hatched under Eisenhower but Kennedy—under a number of misimpressions—approved it; then—fearing another Korea—refused to call in the United States Air Force to help the invaders.

Supreme Court Justice William O. Douglas recalls talking about the Bay of Pigs with the President: "This episode seared him," he said, explaining that Kennedy had not appreciated "the power that these groups had, these various insidious influences of the CIA and the Pentagon, on civilian policy, and I think it raised in his own mind the spectre: Can Jack Kennedy, President of the United States, ever be strong enough to really rule these two powerful agencies; I think it had a profound effect—it shook him up." Douglas also avers that Kennedy "never thought much of the State Department...He told me he took Rusk because he was a good errand boy...Jack was his own Secretary of State and he knew what he wanted to do."

When it came to the business of competing against the Russians in the space race,

Kennedy made it his business to know in detail about the optimum which the United States could hope to achieve. NASA administrator Dr. Wernher Von Braun, director of the George Marshall Space Flight Center, remembers that the president "found it difficult to understand why some people couldn't see the importance of space. He said he wasn't a technical man but to him it was obvious that space was something we simply could not neglect. That we had to be first in space if we wanted to survive as a nation. And that, at the same time, this was a challenge as great as that confronted by the early explorers of the Renaissance...To him space was, as he so aptly put it, 'the new ocean on which we must learn to sail.'"

It should be remembered that the world at large was more preoccupied with the space race than it is today. In 1957 Russia had orbited Sputnik and in 1961 she had sent the first astronaut around the globe. So it was imperative that Alan Shepard make a sub-orbital flight in May. Then, the following February, John Glenn orbited the globe three times in five hours. The museum exhibits depict these triumphs but the oral histories of Shepard and Glenn themselves conjure the sense of what it was like to be there at the center of things. Both men enjoyed weekends with the president at Hyannisport and describe direct, informal relationships with him.

Andrew Minihan, a Kennedy cousin and mayor of New Ross, Ireland, who welcomed the president to the town of his ancestors, recalls:

"So I was waiting at the platform for him...there was a chief of protocol to introduce me to Mr. X, and Mr. C was to introduce me to the President. By this time the President was in sight and the people were shouting their heads off. Immediately after his car arrived, he jumped out of the car and he went straight forward to me and he said, 'Mayor Minihan,' said he, 'my brother (Edward M.) Ted sent you his kindest regards and he said he had a whale of a time with you here in New Ross.' And I knew from that minute that I was speaking to a man...and

112

naturally I fell for him and so did everybody else. I mean, he just had that humanity about him that—what is it (Rudyard) Kipling said? 'To walk with kings and not lose the common touch...'

...Well, when he was finished there...We had been ordered by the American Embassy not to let people shake hands with him because of his back injury. But the man, he himself, wanted to meet the people. When he came down off the platform his bodyguards were trying to push him into the car and he said, 'No, I'm going to meet the people.' So they said, 'Right, sir. Come this way.' And he caught me by the arm and said, 'Mayor, we go this way,' going the opposite way. So he went around amongst the people and everybody was absolutely thrilled with him. He just seemed to exude this feeling of genuineness, you know, and friendliness, and he seemed to be perfectly happy and perfectly at ease."

Princess Grace of Monaco, interviewed by novelist Paul Gallico, June 19, 1965, describes her first meeting with Kennedy in the New York hospital in which the senator had been confined for his back. Mrs. Kennedy and her sister "wanted me to go into his room and say I was the new night nurse" she relates.

"He recognized me at once and couldn't have been sweeter or more quick to put me at my ease...

"He was almost too good to be true...he was just like the all-American boy, wasn't he, handsome, a fighter, witty, full of charm..."

George Smathers reflects:

"One thing about the guy besides his guts, on the one hand, was his total tenderness and sensitivity on the other, which made him a great friend. He was a total realist. I don't have any memory of him kidding himself about anything. I got the feeling he was totally self-confident. He figured if given the opportunity, if given the fact, he could come up with as right a decision as anybody could, but I don't remember that he ever thought he was God's gift to the world or anything like that."

    Senator Edward M. Kennedy giving his remarks at the dedication of the Kennedy Library.

On The Way to Columbia Point

"Someday, it is safe to assume, the seven million Americans who gave for the Kennedy Library will be rewarded with a finished product, and chances are it will all be such a smashing success that memories of the hell involved in getting it built will gradually recede," predicted a Boston Globe reporter in 1970. He was right.

In 1980 the powerfully simple lines of the library, so right in their seascape frame, the easy access to a highway on one hand and a university on the other, all make such obvious sense that the visitor might assume that this is the way Kennedy himself envisioned it. But it wasn't.

In 1961 John F. Kennedy announced his intention to build his presidential library on the banks of the Charles River, overlooking Harvard Universtiy. Harvard president Nathan Pusey had suggested that the president donate his papers to Harvard itself but Kennedy had preferred to follow the lead of his four predecessors in constructing (through public subscription) a presidential library. But while the other Libraries were built at the homes or birthplaces of the men they honor, Kennedy chose to construct his near Harvard. On one hand he had no one home and on the other he would be only fifty-one years old when he retired from his second presidential term in 1969. He hoped to teach at Harvard.

In May, 1963, Kennedy inspected two possible sites for what he conceived as a modest, two-story facility. The space he liked best was on the Cambridge side of the Charles River but it was, unfortunately, occupied by train yards belonging to the city's transit authority (the MBTA).

When President Kennedy returned for a second look at the Library sites in October, the Harvard Band put on a half-time show for him about a presidential library in a car barn. He laughed. He was a realist, one familiar with Massachusetts institutions like the transit authority. He swiftly deduced that these fourteen acres would be expensive and difficult to come by. He settled instead for the 2.2 acre site on the other side of the river in Brighton, near the Harvard Business School, a selection which was formalized within a few days when Harvard agreed to donate the land.

A little more than one month later Kennedy was dead and his family turned to the proposed library as a positive focus for their grief. A campaign to raise six million dollars (twice the amount required for any previous presidential library) was soon launched and construction of the building was scheduled to begin in 1965; it was to be completed in 1968.

Plans for the library were, however, ballooning. At New York's exclusive River Club the Kennedy brothers met with key associates and discussed the library's contents well into a December night. The last thing they wanted, they agreed, was a Taj Mahal. Since the president himself would no longer be animating it there was a consensus that current statesmen should be involved here with Harvard students (ideally also with the general public) on a day-in and out basis. This Kennedy Institute of Politics would be an integral part of Harvard's graduate School of Government (to be renamed in Kennedy's honor).

Next spring, eighteen of the world's most prestigious architects came to town to inspect the two acres. They didn't like the view of the local power station across the river and they agreed that the site was too small, a verdict echoed by I. M. Pei when he became the architect to do the job. It should be noted that while the original concept of the library was already twice as ambitious as the extant presidential libraries that in August, 1965, Lyndon Johnson announced plans for his own library—a vast thirty-five thousand square foot monolith to be built on fourteen acres at the Universtiy of Texas, Austin. Kennedy's memory, it should also be remembered, was still so fresh and powerful that nothing seemed too much to ask in his name.

Nothing else, in fact, could have moved the MBTA car barns, an eye-sore, long resented by Harvard. In October of 1965 the Commonwealth of Massachusetts appropriated seven million dollars to buy the transit authority site and the following March the MBTA agreed to accept $6,098,400 for twelve acres (The Kennedy Library Corporation bought the two remaining acres for the Kennedy Institute). The MBTA agreed to vacate the yards by 1970. This marked the high point of hopes for the library in Cambridge.

It was all downhill for the next five years. First the MBTA failed to find an alternative site for their cars—one community after another rebuffed them. Then when they settled on the Penn Central yards in South Boston (purchased for $6.5 million in 1970) the project continued to stall while construction costs soared. Fund raising officially ceased in 1971 when nineteen million dollars had been accumulated.

In 1970 the groundbreaking date for the Library was pushed back three times, beginning with 1972, ending with 1975.

It was the museum part of the Library which local residents began to object to, complaining that it would draw up to two million tourists a year (a grossly inflated figure) to an already traffic-clogged Harvard Square. The announcement that an eighteen story, three hundred and fifteen unit Holiday Inn was about to be constructed on the edge of the Square confirmed the doomsayers' predictions that the area's low-rise, famously distinctive character would soon vanish.

Polls taken at the time reveal that the Library's opponents never represented more than twenty-five percent of Cambridge residents. But they were an extremely vocal lot.

Unfortunately, it was at this juncture (May, 1973) that I. M. Pei's most controversial design for the site was unveiled. In the nine years since receiving his commission for the Library, Pei had designed two other major projects in Boston; one of them—the city's tallest skyscraper—was having a notoriously hard time keeping its windows in place. The eighty-five foot high glass pyramid which formed the centerpiece for the proposed complex (it was framed on three sides by conventional structures) was thus the butt of much local humor. Pei eventually withdrew the design, submitting a far more subdued one the following year.

Lyndon Johnson's presidential library had opened in May, 1971, but three years later the Kennedy Library was still bogged, quite literally since it had been discovered that it would be grounded in a peat bog, precluding the planned underground garage, giving the local opposition a new parking problem to rally 'round. The General Services Administration commissioned an environmental impact study.

Library Director Dan Fenn has chronicled what happened next:

> In February, 1975, after the release of a controversial environmental impact statement...with protracted and serious litigation in the offing and inflation eating rapidly into the available funds, the Library Corporation announced that it would no longer attempt to build both the library's museum and archives in Cambridge.

The University of Massachusetts responded immediately, inviting the Library to locate either on its Amherst campus (in the Western part of the State) or at its fledgling harborside branch at Columbia Point.

According to Dan Fenn: "That opened a floodgate of invitations—one hundred and seventy-five in all—and the corporation began carefully weighing each one of them, as well as exploring a number of other possible areas in and around Boston."

Washington was also considered but by November the options were narrowed to placing the museum in the Charlestown Navy Yard just north of Boston proper and keeping

116

the archives in Cambridge, or combining the archives and museum in one building at Columbia Point.

Today, this building—far simpler and surer than I. M. Pei's first four designs, is an unchallenged triumph. The Cambridge site today is occupied (at least the two acres purchased by the Kennedy Corporation in 1964) by the Kennedy School of Government (of which the Institute is a part). It is a low key, glass and brick building set back from the street in green lawn.

This site is at the corner of two busy streets. It could never support a building of the majesty which now dominates Columbia Point.

In 1963, when John F. Kennedy first coveted this corner, Columbia Point was still just the name of a blighted housing project and a bleak expanse of land created by decades of dumping. The Universtiy of Massachusetts campus here was but a possibility.

It's little wonder that it took more than sixteen years for even the library plan to move the eight miles from Harvard to the harbor. There are echoes here of the biblical story about the stone rejected by the builders becoming the corner stone of the temple. The library's tortuous route to this place is itself a story which deserves to be remembered, especially in view of the thirty million people from throughout the world who—by contributing to the cost of this building—were as much a part of its struggle as they are of its fruition.

The Kennedy Library sits at the tip of Columbia Point, its glass prow—tinted to reflect the sun—pointing northeast across Dorchester Bay.

117

(Photo: S. Carothers)

A giant American flag is suspended over the glass-walled pavilion of the JFK Library.

A museum visitor is silhouetted against the glass wall of the pavilion, the soaring space through which exhibit goers exit. In the background is JFK's old sailboat "Victura," permanently beached by the library building.

(Photo: S. Carothers)

Architecture

Like a lighthouse the Library looms alone against sea and sky. One day it is a study in white shapes against contrasting blues, the next it is a muted light, wrapped in greys.

Your first impression—as it was of John F. Kennedy—is of a disarmingly open, dynamic presence.

"The library should be a building without a hat," a Kennedy friend remarked back in 1964. It is.

Like Kennedy himself it is also extremely sophisticated. Superficially it appears to be but three simple, geometric shapes—a square (the pavillion), a triangle (the ten-story archives tower), and a circle (the theater). It is actually an orchestration of a half dozen triangles and circles rooted in a subsurface square.

Approaching the library you are preoccupied with its stark, unconventional lines. You barely notice the upward tilt to the road as you pass a small outfall building. Look to your left at this point, however, and you will see the castle-like Calf Pasture Pumping Station, built in 1883 to work a giant sewer pipe which then formed the northern end of this peninsula.

The point is that once you cross this pipe you are on land created less than a decade ago when the University of Massachusetts site was excavated.

The exhibit area is at the existing level of the land (twenty-two feet above sea level) while the entrance level is that of the pipe (thirty-seven feet). Within the building itself the natural slope of the land is retained in the aisles of the movie theaters.

The library is sited with extreme care for its surroundings. One diagonal, for instance, leads to the old pump house, another out to Graves' Light, the outermost beacon in Boston Harbor. As a result the building is at once a foil to and a means of involving you with the water and skyline beyond. Following its angular thrusts and its curves, you find yourself seeing more in the seascape than you would were the building not here.

On entering the library you are confronted immediately with the sweep of Dorchester Bay, all the more enticing since it is viewed from a balcony and through the lattice-work of the pavilion wall beyond.

Next you are in a square anteroom, walled with JFK photos and quotations. There is but one window in this space, a

A wide concrete staircase sweeps down the side of the Kennedy Library to a seaside terrace landscaped like a Cape Cod dune.

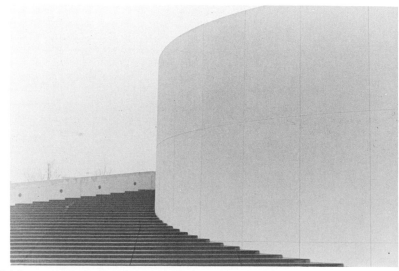

119

six-by-six frame around the president's favorite sailboat, the Victura, which sits on the lawn, slightly heeled and heading out to sea.

For the next hour you are immersed in the Kennedy era, first through the thirty minute film and then through the kaleidoscopic overlays of facts, photos and film clips in the exhibit area—a series of unusual spaces, each designed to suit a chapter in the Kennedy family story, all radiating off the centerpiece exhibit—which sits at the literal center of the building—the replica of the desk at which presidential decisions were made.

It is all overwhelming. Surfeited with facts and visual impressions, you emerge into the emptiness of the vast (seventy by seventy foot) pavilion. After an hour below decks you are suddenly in a soaring glass box thrust, seemingly, right into Dorchester Bay.

The Hancock tower is clearly visible from the library, especially from the Bay Plaza, a triangular space jutting off to star-

board. Just in case the building's lighthouse qualities have escaped you, there is a real beacon here too.

From the Bay Plaza you look back up at the single square window in the anteroom Everything else is chalk white concrete, suggesting sails, banked behind the prow-like glass wall of the pavilion. You are practically forced to gaze out expectantly, as you would from the bow of a ship (the triangular point of land, like that of the pavilion itself, resembles a stylized ship's bow). This is the building's public face.

This rendering of the library is a profile as seen from the west side.

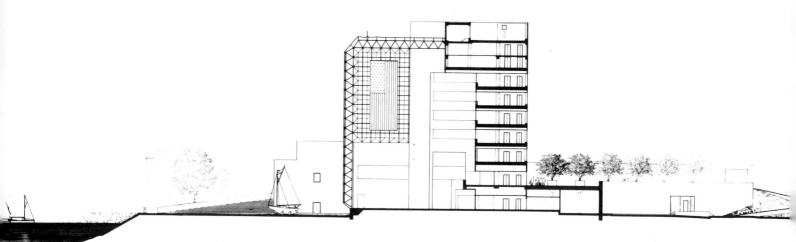

An entrance-level view; here the circle
includes the two theaters and their shared
lobby; the triangle which stands out here
is simply the bookstore area.

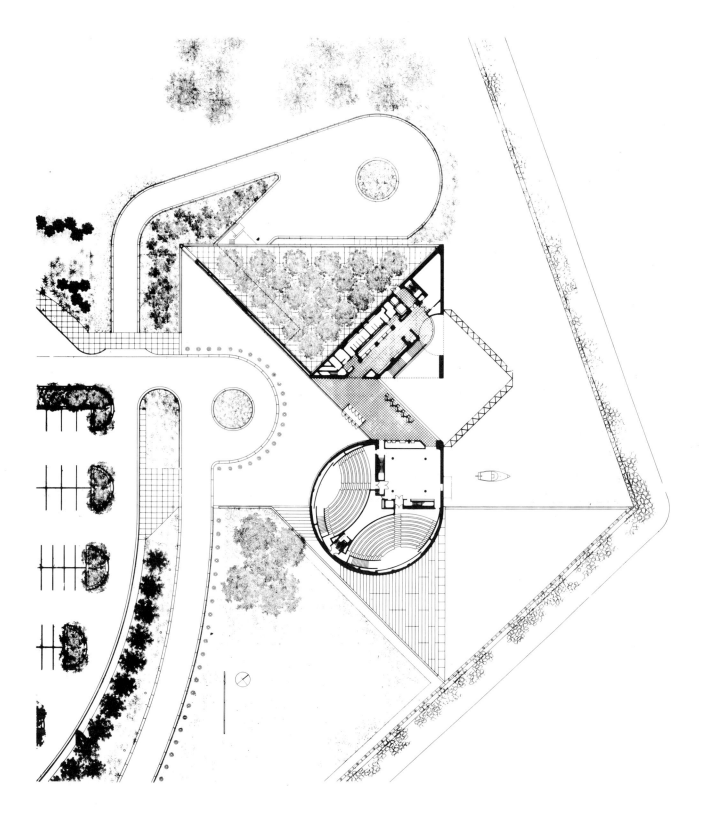

The best view of the archival tower itself is from the sheltered West Plaza, still another triangular space set in the lee of the building, a court-like area graced with wooden benches set below trees which are planted in round, concrete drums. The odd-sized and angled windows here create their own pattern on the concrete wall and the horizontal lines of the railings underscore the line of the shore beyond.

At this writing the foreground here is a no-man's land with only the pump station to see. Within a decade this area will be tidied and developed. But, in contrast to sites proposed for the library in Cambridge, the future building will take shape in relation to this, the commanding presence. Although the library occupies just 9.5 acres of the three hundred and seventy-one acre peninsula it is assured future space to breathe.

In order for the library to stand here in the first place it was necessary to construct a half million dollar "rip-rap," a porous stone wall varying in thickness from eight to fifteen feet, plunging twenty-five feet down; this is a stone sieve meant to dissipate wave pressure. The building itself is set on piles driven one hundred and fifty feet down through the clay into rock. The twenty-two foot exhibit level is, incidentally, 16.5 feet higher than the highest tide recorded in this area.

The library's construction itself was something to see: its white, concrete panels, each weighing more than eight tons, were trucked in miles from western Massachusetts and assembled here like a giant jigsaw.

At this writing the landscaping, with the exception of the sturdy black pines, Cape Cod dune grass and rose bushes—has a way to grow before it effectively anchors the building to its site.

On the other hand, this building will probably never look completely anchored. The more you explore its spaces, both inside and out, the more you are impressed with the fact that this building is never static. Its angles and curves reflect every change in light and its interior spaces are constantly affected by the mood of the seascape beyond its windows. As much as any sculpture in glass and stone is able, this building captures the spirit of the young president who repeatedly urged his country "to move again," to pick up anchor and to set sail.

An exhibit-level rendering. The circular area is the lobby; note the step ramp leading to the Bay Plaza on the lobby's left and the square pavilion set at an angle into the larger square of the exhibit area.

A Fitting Location

There are wonderful ironies in the fact that the Kennedy Library stands at the tip of Columbia Point on Dorchester Bay, not on the banks of the Charles River and by Harvard University.

The Kennedy Library Corporation's decision to build on the bay-side site, was initially rather reluctant and unenthusiastic and for, what seemed to Bostonians anyway, very good reasons. In local minds, Columbia Point was inextricably associated with the crime-ridden and nearly derelict public housing project of the same name. Hardly the suitable place for a memorial to a martyred president and beloved local hero.

But, Columbia Point's dubious reputation—it had been a prison camp and a garbage dump before public housing authorities moved in—obscured its assets and advantages.

It is, for one thing, a very beautiful place in a quite natural way. A mostly manmade peninsula jutting out into Dorchester Bay, it is sun drenched in good weather, wind-whipped almost always so that the air is cool and fresh, redolent of the sea. The view of the bay is marvelous, taking in some of the islands as well and on the horizon the lighthouse that marks the entrance to Boston Harbor: President's Roads.

Boston's great days as a seaport are behind it, but the ship channel is still a busy one and on a fine day you can lean over the railing of the library promenade and watch a procession of yachts, tankers, fishing boats, warships, and freighters sail by.

Not a bad place to remember a sailor president, one who had sailed the sea for pleasure and in war and loved it in all its moods.

There are other aspects of Columbia Point that make it a remarkably apt location for a memorial to JFK. Kennedy was a son of Harvard, and a loyal one, but he was also a public man so there is something fitting about the fact that his library stands in the shade of the modernistic red brick complex of the University of Massachusetts Boston campus, rather than in the shadow of the mellow, ivy-covered brick buildings of less egalitarian Harvard.

And, for a president deeply concerned with the plight of the poor and the decay of American cities there is nothing really unsuitable about the nearby presence of a low income housing project. One of Columbia Point's ironies is that this long neglected facility found itself targeted for massive improvement—part of a seventy-five million dollar program to redevelop the peninsula—just a few months after the Kennedy Library opened.

The plan calls for converting the housing project into a middle income apartment complex, opening a shopping mall, constructing a three-story building adjacent to the library to house Massachusetts State Archives; and building a waterside park with swimming and fishing facilities. It will all take about a decade to complete, but in the end much-maligned Columbia Point will be transformed from a civic embarassment to a desirable neighborhood.

JFK, one suspects, would be pleased at that.

JFK was an historian, and while at first glance Columbia Point doesn't have much history, a second glance is more revealing. There is nothing very historic on the peninsula itself, it's true—unless you count the imposing, romantic revival granite sewage pumping station built in 1883—but history is in view all around it.

Looking Northwest over Boston Harbor from the promenade or pavillion of the library, you can see the honey colored ramparts of Fort Independence, or Castle Island as it is usually called. This has been a bastion since the 1630's, making it the oldest continually fortified spot in the country. During the latter part of the American Revolution, the fort was commanded by no less than Paul Revere.

But, before Revere could take charge, the British had to be persuaded to withdraw. That was done just to the north of Columbia Point, on the high hill in South Boston topped by a monument shaped like a church steeple. This is known as Dorchester Heights and here in the spring of 1776 the Continental Army, commanded by George Washington, mounted heavy guns captured at Fort Ticonderoga in New York the previous year and laboriously hauled to Boston on sleighs.

With the Americans able to fire down on them at will, the British position was untenable and they had to evacuate Boston, which had been under siege for a year. On March 17, 1776, the British sailed away and Boston has celebrated that date ever since as Evacuation Day.

It is also St. Patrick's Day, and South Boston has long been considered the stronghold of the Boston Irish so "The Day" as it known in "Southie" is celebrated with considerable Celtic enthusiasm.

Politics, of course, is also an Irish enthusiasm—one the Kennedys exemplify—and during election years, the South Boston Parade is a political happening attended by almost every Boston pol who seeks office or values reelection. John, Robert, Edward, and their grandfather, Patrick J. Kennedy, all marched in St. Patricks Day parades while "Honey Fitz," their maternal grandfather, as mayor of the city, frequently led them.

To the east, and beyond Dorchester Heights, is the skyline of downtown Boston, a grove of skyscrapers marking the State Street financial district. Just to the west, and a glimmering landmark if the light is right, is the golden dome of the Massachusetts State House.

Kennedy gave one of his finest speeches beneath the dome, an address to the Great and General Court, as Massachusetts terms its state legislature. It was on January 9, 1961 and was the first speech he made after being elected president. He insisted that it was not a farewell: "For forty-three years—whether I was in London or in Washington or in the South Pacific or elsewhere—this has been my home; and God willing, wherever I serve, this shall remain my home."

He called for national greatness on that day, and speaking as a Massachusetts man, quoted the great Puritan leader John Winthrop, governor of the Massachusetts Bay Colony, who told his followers never to forget that: "We must consider that we shall be a city upon a hill. The eyes of all people are upon us..."

A hill that loomed large in the lives of those early Puritans is just to the west of the Kennedy Library across the Southeast Expressway: Savin Hill.

In June of 1630, Puritan settlers who had sailed across from England in the great fleet organized by Winthrop, landed at the foot of the hill and established a settlement, naming it Dorchester after the Dorsetshire town so many of them came from.

The new Dorchester became a town itself but was eventually absorbed by Boston, becoming the city's largest neighborhood. Dorchester was one of the areas that Irish-Americans moved to when they prospered and left their original immigrant enclaves. The Fitzgerald family had a handsome house in the Ashmont section of Dorchester, just southwest of Savin Hill, and Rose Kennedy grew up there.

The Kennedy Library faces the sea, but at an angle that points it toward Boston Light, a northwesterly course roughly paralleling the one taken by Patrick Kennedy in 1846 when he sailed for America. A humble cooper, he was part of the historic exodus caused by the Irish potato famine, "The Great Hunger," a mass movement that was to have a greater impact on Boston than on any other city. But, few immigrants were to have quite the impact Patrick did.

So, for a number of reasons and in several ways, Columbia Point seems indeed a fitting place for John Fitzgerald Kennedy to have his library.

"Jack's library and this site were made for each other," Senator Edward Kennedy said at the ground breaking ceremonies in 1977. Most visitors agree.

Outreach

There were probably more speeches delivered for the dedication of the John F. Kennedy Library than for any other public building in America.

In conjunction with the dedication on October 20, 1979 a group of seventy-five men and women, prominent in national affairs, visited some seventy high schools in Greater Boston, Central and Western Massachusetts, Maine, Vermont, and Rhode Island and talked about American government in general and John and Robert Kennedy in particular.

Speakers included political figures such as Senator Edward M. Kennedy, George McGovern, and Henry Cabot Lodge; academics such as John Kenneth Galbraith, Arthur Schlesinger, and Richard Neustadt; and journalists like Theodore White, Anthony Lewis and Art Buchwald.

The company was as distinguished as the program was novel. All the speakers attended the actual dedication, their presence attesting to a determination to make the Kennedy Library not just a repository of records and memories, but a living institution reaching out to the world around it as well as welcoming visitors who pass through its doors.

"We are a unique kind of institution, one not fixed in tradition...and we are trying to use John F. Kennedy's life in a way that illustrates politics and American government," said John F. Stewart, assistant director for education of the Kennedy Library.

Others may perceive it as a memorial to a martyred president or a political science and history research facility, but the Kennedy Library intends to become a significant educational institution. And, it is one that doesn't lack for students. School groups are among the most frequent visitors to the library and in the first year of operation about one thousand students on average trooped through the library museum each week.

After touring the museum, school groups usually hear a talk from a staff member and get to ask questions. They also often get to be president of the United States—at least to feel what it is like to make presidential decisions. To help young visitors appreciate some of the problems of the presidency, the library has developed several "decision games" in which participants have to pretend that they are sitting in the Oval Office when a tough presidential decision is called for.

The most popular, "Go-No Go," involves a 1961 Kennedy decision to approve the first space flight by an American astronaut. The arguments not to go—presented by a Kennedy Library staff member, in the role of a presidential advisor—are strong: There are more important national concerns than the space race; there is a risk that the astronaut will be killed, a disaster would kill the whole space program, instruments can do the job, particularly since the Russians have already demonstrated by their successful manned flight that human beings can withstand weightlessness. But, the arguments for "Go" are equally compelling: The nation needs a psychological lift, the U. S. image abroad was damaged when the Russians moved ahead in the space race and Americans would respond to the challenge to be Number 1 again; there is only a one in ten risk of an accident, one the astronauts are willing to take; and Congress, which has been lukewarm to most New Frontier programs, wants a space success.

Few of the students who play the "Go-No-Go" game were alive in 1961. But they almost always decide—as JFK did—to send a man into space. (Alan Shepard rocketed one hundred and fifteen miles into the upper atmosphere and returned safely to earth.) Surprisingly, teachers and other older participants who remember the actual event, quite often vote "No Go."

Another decision game involves the use of a film made by the library called "The Stroke of a Pen." It's about JFK's decision to end racial discrimination in federal housing programs by executive order. The film presents the technical, administrative and political problems—there is a Congressional election coming up which JFK had to weigh. The film stops and viewers each decide. They vote overwhelmingly to end discrimination in housing, but generally are divided on just when to do it.

Kennedy waited until after the election, and then signed the order just before Thanksgiving when it attracted a minimum of attention.

These contrasting presidential actions, one deliberately dramatic to rally the country, the other skillfully downplayed to aid a minority—without politically alienating a majority—offer a real insight into the way the American political process works.

Standing alone at the end of Columbia Point, which juts out into Dorchester Bay, the Kennedy Library is a striking sight from whatever angle you view it.

(Photo: S. Carothers)

For very young visitors the museum exhibits are presented as a scavenger hunt for specific items like JFK's christening gown, the model of the PT-109, a piece of moon rock and such. There is even a Kennedy crossword puzzle!

The archives are, of course, a magnet for serious scholars from around the world. But the library takes special pains to attract undergraduates from area colleges and universities. An advisory committee composed of local university professors helps plan periodic conferences to familiarize their colleagues with the wealth of curriculum material to be found here. Political science seminars are held in the Library itself and there are also special film series, lectures and even internships geared to Boston's sizeable undergraduate population.

The third floor research room actually resembles a college library more than anything. Researchers are not allowed to remove books or other materials but they do have access to all unclassified material and they can browse through open shelves containing the world's most comprehensive collection of published works on the Kennedy era; many volumes on the American presidency and recent American history are included.

Documents may not be removed, but they can be copied. As an aid to novice researchers, the education department has put together a packet consisting of some four hundred documents relating to the mental retardation policies of the Kennedy administration. Letters, memos, reports, etc., these are the kinds of material that a skilled researcher would cull from the archives after prolonged, patient work.

Along with a kit which consists of an entire week's worth of presidential papers, this is geared to highschool students. Orientation programs, along with curriculum workshops and lectures, are held specifically for highschool teachers too.

John Stewart stresses that "Although organized school groups occupy most of our attention right now, someday there will be programs for all adults who are anxious to learn more about the political world of which they are a part." In November of 1980 a series of Neighborhood Forums, part of Boston's three hundred and fiftieth birthday celebration, were held at the Library to examine the way in which local organization influence political decisions.

Not all the Library's outreach programs are about politics. The Ernest Hemingway papers are here too and in July of 1980 a fullscale conference on this outstanding American novelist was held here and on an offshore island.

John Stewart heads a small staff and has a budget for educational projects of about one hundred thousand dollars a year, funded about equally by government appropriation and the Library trust fund, derived from admissions and gift shop sales. "If we had more money we could do more things," he admits.

The outreach effort continues to gather steam. At present, a puppet show is in the works, one which will bring political ideas—such as the right to petition the government for a redress of grievances—to young children.

Says Stewart: "We feel that we have something to contribute to the understanding that people of all ages have about politics and government."

Posters, pins, flags, buttons, books and other John and Robert Kennedy memorabilia are sold at the Kennedy Library gift shop. Among the popular items are models of PT-109, kits for making the pillows on the presidential rocking chair, and copies of JFK letters, such as the youthful one in which he petitioned his father for a raise in his allowance.